# 世界名人智慧菁華
## 中英對照

王壽來 輯譯

九歌文庫940

# 象牙塔外的智慧

　　人生多憂患，所以俗諺有「世事不如意者十常八九」、古詩有「生年不滿百，常懷千歲憂」之說。人活在滾滾紅塵中，面對國家的興亡盛衰、萬物的成住壞空，都不可能不心有所感，更甭說直接攸關個人前途的成敗禍福了。所以，佛家教人要做到「無我相、無人相、無眾生相、無壽者相」，方能直證菩提，永離苦海，但此一「應無所住而生其心」的境界，世上又有幾人能夠參透？

　　好在，古往今來卻有無數智者，以其深厚的學養、敏銳的觀察，說過許多激勵人心、揭示人生哲理的話語，而這些有若吉光片羽的精采之言，往往是他們總結其一生悲歡離合故事的經驗之談，不僅可以化解人們心中的塊壘，減輕人們心中的苦痛，甚至還能替人們開闢一方可以徜徉其間的心靈淨土，因而，值得你我視其為一生一世可以相守、永不遺忘的座右銘。

　　舉例而言，凡是讀過當代美國小說家艾爾邦（Mitch Albom）所寫的暢銷書《在天堂遇見的五個人》（The Five People You Meet in Heaven）的人，一定很難忘記書中的這一段令人動容的話：

　　　　失去的愛，仍舊是愛，它只是以不同的形式存在罷了。你無法看到他們的微笑，或帶給他們食物，或輕撫他們的髮絲，抑或在舞池中翩翩共舞。但是，當那些感覺減弱，另一種感覺卻變強了，那就是記憶，記憶變成你的拍檔，你滋養它，擁抱它，與其跳舞。生命必定有結束之時，愛卻不然。

　　　　Lost love is still love. It takes a different form,

that's all. You can't see their smile or bring them
food or tousle their hair or move them around a dance
floor. But when those senses weaken another heightens.
Memory. Memory becomes your partner. You nurture it.
You hold it. You dance with it. Life has to end, love
doesn't.

對許多人來說，失去的真愛，不論是親情、友情或愛情，
永遠是心中永難癒合的傷口，不管歷經多少時日、多少歲月，
每一觸及，仍有餘痛。面對這樣的人生缺憾，有些人求助於心
理醫生，有些人尋求宗教信仰的慰藉，有些人認命而默默接受
命運的擺佈。

儘管如此，當我們接觸到艾爾邦前述經典之語，或許並無
當頭棒喝之感，然而，那種長久鬱結於心、無以言宣的感傷，
無形中竟獲得了解脫。我們不難發現，智者之言，像是熠熠明
燈，照亮人生的道路；它又像是和煦的春暉，溫暖人們的心
靈；更像是晨曦的第一道曙光，點燃我們對生命的熱情與希
望。

智者之言，正如那首表達感恩之情的英文歌《你將我舉
起》（You Raise Me Up）中所述：「你將我舉起，讓我站在群
山之巔；你將我舉起，讓我走在暴風雨的海上；當我站在你的
肩上，我是何等堅強；你將我舉起，讓我超越自己。」

翻閱本書，不論哪一頁，一定都會有觸動你心靈的智者之
言，你將發現，只要自己願意走出生命的象牙塔，不管行腳何
方，處處可見生活的智慧。你也不難發現，自己在世上活得並
不孤獨，因為畢竟還有人真正瞭解你的內心世界，也說出了你
不輕易與人分享的感受。

衷心感謝九歌出版社的負責人蔡文甫大哥，以及總編輯陳
素芳小姐，沒有他們的慧眼，這本勵志類譯作就不可能問世。

英國十九世紀的作家科爾頓（Charles Caleb Colton）說得好：「寫作有三難：寫值得出版的東西、找到誠實的人出版、擁有明智的人去閱讀。」對這三者我都有信心，其中第二項更不在話下！

王壽來 二〇一〇年十月

## 企管界

## 音樂界

## 政治界

# 文學界

## 思想界

## 社會賢達

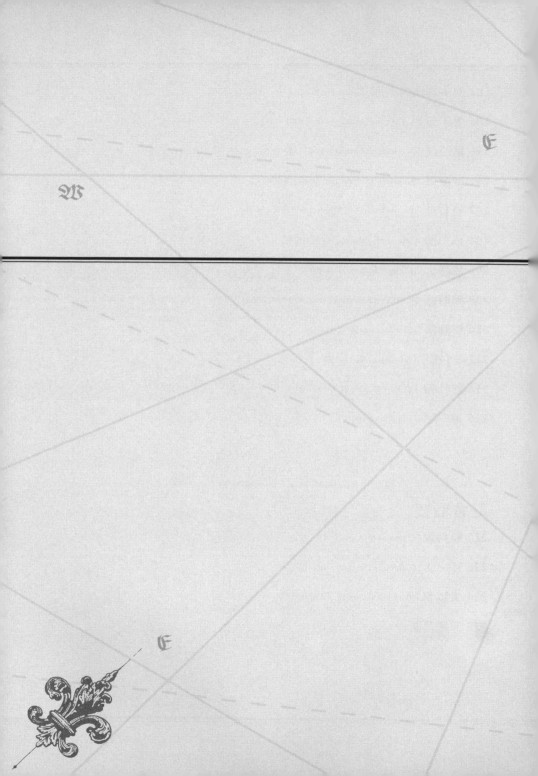

# 藝術界

# 杜布菲 (Jean Dubuffet, 1901-1985)

法國當代藝術大師級畫家、雕刻家和版畫家,第二次世界大戰後巴黎畫派的主將。首先利用廢棄物從事創作,1940年代末形成自己的風格,稱為原生藝術(Art Brut),強調揚棄傳統藝術形式,以發自內心的原始欲望及直覺來進行創作。杜氏不以抽象或具象來歸類其作品,一般藝術史將他歸類於「無形式主義」。作品有《地下鐵》、《貴婦的身軀》等。

● 對我來說,瘋狂反是超級理智。正常人個個頭腦不清;正常,意味著缺乏想像、缺乏創意。

For me, insanity is super sanity. The normal is psychotic. Normal means lack of imagination, lack of creativity.

● 藝術是訴求於心靈,而非眼睛。原始人類一直就是如此看待藝術,而他們是對的。藝術是一種語言、知識的工具、溝通的工具。

Art addresses itself to the mind, and not to the eyes. It has always been considered in this way by primitive peoples, and they are right. Art is a language, instrument of knowledge, instrument of communication.

● 藝術不會躺在鋪好的床上;一有人提到它的名字,它馬上開溜。藝術喜歡隱姓埋名,它的最好時光,就在它忘記自己的稱呼之時。

Art does not lie down on the bed that is made for it; it runs away as soon as one says its name; it loves to be incognito. Its best moments are when it forgets what it is called.

● 藝術是人類能力所及的盡情宣洩。

Art is the most passionate orgy within man's grasp.

- 我個人非常相信野蠻的價值；我所指的是：直覺、激情、情緒、暴力、瘋狂。

  Personally, I believe very much in values of savagery; I mean: instinct, passion, mood , violence, madness.


- 我期待在任何一件藝術作品上，看到的是令我驚奇的東西，它要違反我對事物通常的評量，代之以其他意想不到的角度。

  What I expect from any work of art is that it surprises me, that it violates my customary valuations of things and offers me other, unexpected ones.


- 藝術必須讓你感到有點好笑，同時感到有點害怕，只要不讓你厭煩，無所不可。

  Art must make you laugh a little and make you a little afraid. Anything as long as it doesn't bore.


- 讓我們揚棄過去，以及過去的一切！讓我們從事藝術創作，好像人類從未創作過那樣。

  Let us abolish the past, and all that comes with it! And let us make art as if no human being had ever made it before.

# 波洛克 (Jackson Pollock, 1912-1956)

美國畫家，抽象表現主義運動的領航者，對現代西方藝術的發展有重大影響。抽象表現主義在美國是以行動繪畫的形式著稱，波洛克所發展的「滴畫技法」，成為波氏戛戛獨造的創作標記。作品有《鳥》、《男人與女人》、《祕密的捍衛者》、《肖像與夢境》、《復活節與圖騰》、《陰暗海洋》、《深》、《白光》和《芳香》等。

● 在我看來，現代藝術家就是在營造與表現一個內在的世界，換言之，乃在表現其活力、動向以及其他的內在力量。

The modern artist, it seems to me, is working and expressing an inner world, in other words—expressing the energy, the motion and other inner forces.

● 只要有訊息傳達，顏料如何塗抹，並無多大關係。技巧只是表述的一種方法而已。

It doesn't make much difference how the paint is put on as long as something has been said. Technique is just a means of arriving at a statement.

● 繪畫是自我發現，優秀的藝術家個個都能畫出自己是怎樣的人。

Painting is self-discovery. Every good artist paints what he is.

● 抽象畫是抽象的，與你相沖。不久前有一位評論家寫說，我的畫無始亦無終，他無意恭維我，但那卻是一種恭維。

Abstract painting is abstract. It confronts you. There was a reviewer a while back who wrote that my pictures didn't have any beginning or any end. He didn't mean it as a compliment, but it was.

- 我在作畫時，並不清楚自己在做什麼。只有在經過一段熟悉期之後，我才能看出一個所以然來。我並不害怕改變，因為畫作有其本身的生命。

  When I'm painting, I'm not aware of what I'm doing. It's only after a get acquainted period that I see what I've been about. I've no fears about making changes for the painting has a life of its own.

- 在地板上，我更感到自在，我感覺更接近、更屬於那張畫，因為這樣子我可以繞著畫走，從四邊工作，簡直就是人在畫中。

  On the floor I am more at ease. I feel nearer, more part of the painting, since this way I can walk around it, work from the four sides and literally be in the painting.

- 現代畫家是用空間與時間來創作，表達的是其感情，而不是在從事圖解。

  The modern artist is working with space and time, and expressing his feelings rather than illustrating.

- 這種陌生感終會消除，我想我們會發現現代藝術的深層意義。

  The strangeness will wear off and I think we will discover the deeper meanings in modern art.

- 在回答提問：「你怎麼知道何時才算完成畫作？」波洛克答說：「你怎麼知道何時結束做愛？」

  In response to the question "How do you know when you're finished?", Pollock replied "How do you know when you're finished making love?"

# 黛安阿巴斯（Diane Arbus, 1923-1971）

美國新紀實攝影最重要的旗手，也是20世紀公認的攝影大師，慣將畸形人、變性人、流浪漢、同性戀者、裸體主義者、智障者等社會邊緣人納入鏡頭，作為創作的主題來進行探索。她是美國第一位參加威尼斯藝術雙年展的攝影家，被藝壇推崇為攝影界的「梵谷」，一生追求「不正常」的影像，最終以自殺結束其如日中天的攝影生命。

- 一張照片是一則有關祕密的祕密，它告訴你的愈多，你知道的愈少。

  A photograph is a secret about a secret. The more it tells you the less you know.

- 我從未拍出我原想拍出的照片，它們不是較好就是較壞。

  I never have taken a picture I've intended. They're always better or worse.

- 我工作起來每每手忙腳亂，我的意思是我不喜歡安排事物，我若站在某樣東西前面，我不會去安排它，而是安排自己。

  I work from awkwardness. By that I mean I don't like to arrange things. If I stand in front of something, instead of arranging it, I arrange myself.

- 愛情涉及一種「瞭解」與「誤解」的奇妙結合。

  Love involves a peculiar unfathomable combination of understanding and misunderstanding.

- 你在街上看到某人，情不自禁的，你所注意到的就是其缺陷。

  You see someone on the street, and essentially what you notice about them is the flaw.

- 我真的相信，有些東西若非我把它們攝影下來，沒人會注意得到。

  I really believe there are things nobody would see if I didn't photograph them.

- 不管你內心如何感覺，一定要努力表現得像贏家，就算你已落後，一種泰然自若與信心滿滿的鎮定神情，會讓你擁有導致勝利的心理優勢。

  Regardless of how you feel inside, always try to look like a winner. Even if you are behind, a sustained look of control and confidence can give you a mental edge that results in victory.

- 世界只能靠行動來掌握，而不能靠思考；手是心靈的前哨。

  The world can only be grasped by action, not by contemplation. The hand is the cutting edge of the mind.

- 大多數人一生都在怕受到傷害，怪人生來就有其創傷，他們已通過人生的考驗，他們是貴族。

  Most people go through life dreading they'll have a traumatic experience. Freaks were born with their trauma. They've already passed their test in life. They're aristocrats.

- 世上沒有比自欺更為順理成章，一個人心有所盼，也就會信以為真。

  Nothing is easier than self-deceit. For what each man wishes, that he also believes to be true.

# 安迪沃荷（Andy Warhol, 1928-1987）

美國藝術家、電影製片人、普普藝術運動的先鋒。擅用通俗詼諧的語言，解構組成生活的元素。他利用照相絲漏版大量製作消費品的圖片，真實反映出美國物質文明的空虛，亦為美國的商業文化開拓了新的疆域。1960年代，沃荷專注於電影製片，作品常被歸為地下電影。從70年代起直至去世，他不斷製作政界及好萊塢名人圖像，也從事廣告繪圖及其他商業藝術計畫。

- 賺錢是藝術，工作是藝術，生意興隆是一切的最高藝術。

  Making money is art and working is art and good business is the best art of all.

- 普普藝術是給每一個人的，我不認為藝術只應為選定的少數人存在。

  Pop art is for everyone. I don't think art should be only for the select few.

- 繪畫太麻煩，機器較少問題，我願自己是一部機器，我認為人人都應該是一部機器。

  Paintings are too hard. Machines have less problems. I'd like to be a machine. I think everybody should be a machine.

- 我喜歡空白牆壁，牆上只要一掛東西，就顯得醜陋。

  I like empty walls. As soon as you put something on them they look terrible.

- 在未來的世界裡，每個人只能成名十五分鐘。

  In the future everyone will be famous for fifteen minutes.

- 今天我打破了東西，才領悟到，我應該每星期打破一次東西……以提醒自己生命何其脆弱。

  I broke something today, and I realized I should break something once a week...to remind me how fragile life is.


- 出生於世，一若遭人綁票，然後被賣為奴。

  Being born is like being kidnapped. And then sold into slavery.


- 自從電影問世以來，就真正主導了美國的一切。電影告訴你要做什麼、如何做、何時做、如何感受，以及如何看待你的感受。

  It's the movies that have really been running things in America ever since they were invented. They show you what to do, how to do it, when to do it, how to feel about it, and how to look how you feel about it.


- 所謂藝術家，就是製造人們用不著的東西之人。

  An artist is somebody who produces things that people don't need to have.


- 愛情與性可以並存，有性而沒有愛情可以湊合，有愛情而沒有性也可湊合，但自戀與自淫，卻是不堪聞問的。

  Love and sex can go together and sex and unlove can go together and love and unsex can go together. But personal love and personal sex is bad.

# 艾利 ( Alvin Ailey, 1931-1989 )

美國非洲裔現代舞蹈家，所創立之舞團成為世界上引領風騷的頂尖舞團。舞作無不巧妙的融合古典與現代、爵士、藍調、民謠等。生前榮獲全美有色人種特殊成就獎、甘迺迪中心終身成就獎等深具意義之獎座。其舞團更在2002年贏得布希總統頒贈國家藝術獎（National Medal of Arts），足見艾氏對現代舞及黑人文化之貢獻與影響。

● 從事舞蹈，必須對舞蹈著迷；不是玩票而已，而須全心全意投入。

You have to be obsessed with dance to do dance; it's not something you play with. The commitment must be there, and the involvement total.

● 舞蹈屬於大眾，我相信舞蹈來自於人群，永遠應回歸人群。

Dance is for everybody. I believe that the dance came from the people and that it should always be delivered back to the people.

● 創作過程不是受控於一個你可以任意開關的開關，而是無時無刻的與你同在。

The creative process is not controlled by a switch you can simply turn on or off; it's with you all the time.

● 我們仍得花較多的時間在籌款上，而不是在排練室中從事創作。

We still spend more time chasing funds than we do in the studio in creative work.

- 我正努力向世界表達，我們全是人類，膚色並不重要，重要的是工作品質。

  I am trying to show the world that we are all human beings and that color is not important. What is important is the quality of our work.

- 人們認為，因為舞團看起來很不錯，就表示萬事亨通，他們絕不明白張羅這一切要花多少錢。

  People think that because the company is looking wonderful, everything is fine. They never realize how much all this costs.

- 從事此一行業，生活變成一場長期募款活動。

  In this business, life is one long fund-raising effort.

- 有時候你對自己很不滿意，卻毫無來由。

  Sometimes you feel bad about yourself when there's no reason to.

- 如果你生活在舞蹈的精英世界，你會發現自己是處在充滿種族歧視的世界。

  If you live in the elite world of dance, you find yourself in a world rife with racism.

- 舞蹈訴諸於每個人。

  Dance speaks to everyone.

# 亞曼尼 (Giorgio Armani, 1934- )

義大利服裝設計師，時尚界大師級人物。所推出的男裝，每每引領時尚風潮，堪稱是全球最頂尖之品牌。他設計出結構不完全的外套、簡潔的晚禮服，使時裝不只是追求創意，且能具有實用價值。尤值一提者，是其偏向中性化的設計風格，讓無數愛好者為之傾倒，成為世界各地高層主管和好萊塢明星心目中的最愛。

- 其實我很高興人們能買亞曼尼，就算它是仿冒也罷。我對自己受到舉世歡迎感到欣慰。

  Actually I am very glad that people can buy Armani - even if it's a fake. I like the fact that I'm so popular around the world.

- 我相信我的衣服能讓人們有較好的形象，它可以增加自信與幸福感。

  I believe that my clothes can give people a better image of themselves - that it can increase their feelings of confidence and happiness.

- 我為活生生的世人設計，時時刻刻都以顧客為念，若去開發不實用的衣服或配件，那就沒什麼意義了。

  I design for real people. I think of our customers all the time. There is no virtue whatsoever in creating clothing or accessories that are not practical.

- 我喜歡歷久不衰的東西，也就是那種不過時、禁得起時間考驗、成為絕佳範例的東西。

  I love things that age well - things that don't date, that stand the test of time and that become living examples of the absolute best.

- 我是一名旁觀者，樂於傾聽，而非公開的自我表述，這是多年來我一直保有的特質。

  I was an observer. I liked to listen rather than openly express myself. This trait is something that I've retained over the years.

- 要想創作出與眾不同的東西，心態上必須義無反顧地專注於細枝末節上。

  To create something exceptional, your mindset must be relentlessly focused on the smallest detail.

- 不管你是做好事或壞事，總有異議之聲，甚至就算你在從事公益，人們還會說你是為了做秀。

  There are always protests, whether you do something good or bad. Even if you do something beneficial, people say you do it because it's advertising.

- 風格與時尚的區別，就在於品質。

  The difference between style and fashion is quality.

- 牛仔褲代表著時裝的民主化。

  Jeans represent democracy in fashion.

- 配件是重要的，而且其重要性與日俱增。

  Accessories are important and becoming more and more important every day,

# 聖羅蘭 (Yves Saint Laurent, 1936-2008)

當代法國時裝設計師，以設計各種女裝而聞名於世。17歲時就受到時裝大師迪奧（Christian Dior）的青睞，雇為助手，1957年迪奧過世，公司由其接手。1962年自創品牌，成為巴黎最具影響力之服裝設計師。70年代起，他將營業範圍擴至各種成衣、服裝配件、香水等。

● 我始終相信，流行服飾不僅使女性更美麗，也可使她們感到踏實，給她們信心。

I have always believed that fashion was not only to make women more beautiful, but also to reassure them, give them confidence.

● 我努力呈現流行服飾是一種藝術，為此，我聽從老師克里斯汀迪奧的忠告，以及香奈兒小姐不朽的訓誡，我為我的時代開創新河，而且試著預測明日的趨勢。

I tried to show that fashion is an art. For that, I followed the counsel of my master Christian Dior and the imperishable lesson of Mademoiselle Chanel. I created for my era and I tried to foresee what tomorrow would be.

● 能夠裝扮一名女性的最美衣服，就是她所愛男人的臂膀，但對那些還沒有運氣找到此種幸福的人，還有我在。

The most beautiful clothes that can dress a woman are the arms of the man she loves. But for those who haven't had the fortune of finding this happiness, I am there.

● 時尚會退流行，但風格卻能垂之久遠。

Fashions fade, style is eternal.

- 我要感謝所有穿過我衣服的女性，不管是名人或不是名人，她們對我始終忠心耿耿，帶給我莫大快慰。

  I want to thank all the women who have worn my clothes, the famous and the unknown, who have been so faithful to me and given me so much joy.

- 我真希望是我創造出藍色牛仔褲，它們有表現力、樸實、性感、簡潔，無一不是我希望在我的衣服中所具有的。

  I wish I had invented blue jeans. They have expression, modesty, sex appeal, simplicity - all I hope for in my clothes.

- 經過這些年，我已領悟到，對一件衣服而言，要緊的是穿它的女人。

  Over the years I have learned that what is important in a dress is the woman who is wearing it.

- 我們絕不可把優雅與派頭混為一談。

  We must never confuse elegance with snobbery.

- 打扮是一種生活方式。

  Dressing is a way of life.

# 崔拉夏普 (Twyla Tharp, 1941- )

美國舞蹈家、藝術指導、編舞家。1963年入保羅泰勒舞蹈團，1965年開始從事編舞工作，並自組舞團，不斷創造新的舞蹈語彙。1981年獲舞蹈雜誌獎。1988年加入美國芭蕾舞劇院，成為常駐編舞家。曾獲麥克阿瑟獎、東尼獎，以及兩次艾美獎，長期以來經常指導世界各地舞團，引領現代舞之風潮。著有《創意習慣》等書。

● 藝術，是唯一不必離家的「逃家」方式。

Art is the only way to run away without leaving home.

● 跳舞就像搶劫銀行，分秒必爭。

Dancing is like bank robbery; it takes split-second timing.

● 不少人認定現代舞與芭蕾舞之間有一道牆，我漸漸覺得，所謂的牆是很不健康的東西。

A lot of people insisted on a wall between modern dance and ballet. I'm beginning to think that walls are very unhealthy things.

● 我常說，從事編舞，可以打造出一個行事合乎道德、合乎民主、合乎誠信的世界。

I often say that in making dances I can make a world where I think things are done morally, done democratically, done honestly.

● 舞蹈從來就不是一種特別安逸的生活，這一點人盡皆知。

Dance has never been a particularly easy life, and everybody knows that.

- 我非得對「現代舞蹈」一詞提出質疑不可，對於我所從事的工作，我根本不會使用此一用語，我只是把它視為跳舞、視為移動。

  I would have to challenge the term, modern dance. I don't really use that term in relation to my work. I simply think of it as dancing. I think of it as moving.

- 就是這個不通的用語「後現代主義」，把「現代」這樣一個挺好的詞彙予以摧毀，而「現代」一詞現在已不具任何意義了。

  There's this expression called postmodernism, which is kind of silly, and destroys a perfectly good word called modern, which now no longer means anything.

- 唯一比改變更讓我感到害怕的東西，就是一成不變。固定不變的動作使我抓狂。

  The only thing I fear more than change is no change. The business of being static makes me nuts.

- 我想人們很想把自己的生活簡化到可以掌控的地步，好讓晚上得以安眠。

  I think people want very much to simplify their lives enough so that they can control the things that make it possible to sleep at night.

# 萊柏維茲 ( Annie Leibovitz, 1949- )

美國當代最富傳奇的女性攝影師，也是二十世紀世界最偉大的攝影師之一。1970年代，已嶄露頭角，成為著名音樂雜誌《滾石》（Rolling Stone）的攝影師。1983年，更成為《浮華世界》（Vanity Fair）首席攝影師，亦長期為《時尚》（Vogue）供稿。她擅長用照片說故事，無數經典人物照都出自其手，而除了名人肖像外，她也拍攝過不少戰爭題材。

- 我希望一切有關大自然的壯麗、大地的感動、地方的活力都能留影下來。

  I wish that all of nature's magnificence, the emotion of the land, the living energy of place could be photographed.

- 電腦攝影不是我們所認知的攝影，我認為攝影向來就是化學產物。

  Computer photography won't be photography as we know it. I think photography will always be chemical.

- 在人像攝影中，你有表達觀點的空間，影像未見得就是實相，而是象徵性的東西。

  In a portrait, you have room to have a point of view. The image may not be literally what's going on, but it's representative.

- 照相機使你忘記自身的存在，你不是在躲藏，而是渾然忘我，專注於觀察。

  The camera makes you forget you're there. It's not like you are hiding but you forget, you are just looking so much.

- 攝影家為何不太擅於言談，其中必有道理，我想我們是變懶了。

  There must be a reason why photographers are not very good at verbal communication. I think we get lazy.

- 年輕時，照相機就像朋友，讓你不管行腳何處都覺得有人同行，好像有同伴一般。

  When you are younger, the camera is like a friend and you can go places and feel like you're with someone, like you have a companion.

- 我不認為留白有什麼不好，在我看來，空白牆面並不是問題。

  I don't think there is anything wrong with white space. I don't think it's a problem to have a blank wall.

- 我的希望就是，對自己所熱愛的地方不斷付出，但也關注我們周遭之外的世界。

  My hope is that we continue to nurture the places that we love, but that we also look outside our immediate worlds.

- 目前我所感興趣的是風景，也就是無人的圖畫，要是有一天我的圖像中完全不見人影，我也不會覺得意外。

  What I am interested in now is the landscape. Pictures without people. I wouldn't be surprised if eventually there are no people in my pictures.

- 我仍然需要照相機，因為那是任何人要跟我對話的唯一理由。

  I still need the camera because it is the only reason anyone is talking to me.

# 卡普爾 (Anish Kapoor, 1954- )

英籍印度裔雕塑家。1990年，代表英國參加威尼斯雙年展，榮獲國際評審小組頒發的「Premio 2000」大獎；1992年的《墜入地獄》成為第九屆德國卡塞爾文件大展最受矚目之作。2004年的《雲門》，已是芝加哥的地標。2006年完成的《天鏡》，佇立於紐約第五大道洛克菲勒中心前，備獲佳評。

● 我們不是在為他人創作，即使我非常看重觀眾。

One doesn't make art for other people, even though I am very concerned with the viewer.

● 藝術家並不創作物件，藝術家創作神話。

Artists don't make objects. Artists make mythologies.

● 我覺得對藝術家來說，象徵的世界乃是問題的核心。

I feel the symbolic world is the nub of a problem for an artist.

● 畢卡索所給予自己的那種自由，亦即以千變萬化之姿做一位藝術家，可說是一種極大的心理解放。

That freedom that Picasso afforded himself, to be an artist in a huge number of ways, seems to be a huge psychological liberation.

● 當藝術家是一場漫長的賽事，不是一場十年賽而已，我希望到我八十歲時仍在創作。

Being an artist is a very long game. It is not a 10-year game. I hope I'll be around making art when I'm 80.

- 我的首展在前三分鐘售罄，然後我回到工作室，消耗兩年半的時間幾乎一事無成。

  My first show sold within the first 3 minutes, and I came back to the studio and spent the next two and a half years making almost nothing.

- 大部分我的創作，都是幾何的，就作品的形式而言，可說有一種數學的邏輯。

  Much of what I make is geometric, and has a kind of almost mathematical logic to the form.

- 我想我對空間多少有所瞭解，我認為一名雕塑家的工作，是要把空間與形式的重要性等量齊觀。

  I think I understand something about space. I think the job of a sculptor is spatial as much as it is to do with form.

- 終究，我還是在為自己創作。

  I, in the end, make art for myself.

- 一切觀念無不是來自其他觀念。

  All ideas grow out of other ideas.

# 華特森 ( Bill Watterson, 1958- )

美國當代著名漫畫家。成名之作《凱文的幻虎世界》，是美國的經典連環漫畫，曾在全球 2400家報紙連載。歷年作品出版有16冊單行本，發行20餘國，全球銷售逾3000萬冊。1986年，以28歲之年獲得全美漫畫家協會所頒象徵最高榮譽的魯班獎（Reuben Award），成為史上該獎最年輕的得主。他在1995年宣佈封筆。

● 如果人們夜夜坐在戶外，仰望星辰，我敢說他們會活出另一番境界。

If people sat outside and looked at the stars each night, I'll bet they'd live a lot differently.

● 知道有多玄嗎？日復一日，似乎一無改變，然而轉瞬間，事事全非。

Know what's weird? Day by day, nothing seems to change. But pretty soon, everything's different.

● 我想我們作夢，就可不必久離，設若我們會出現在彼此的夢中，就能通宵同樂。

I think we dream so we don't have to be apart so long. If we're in each other's dreams, we can play together all night.

● 人往往要遭逢一些不幸，才能讓自己活在現實之中，進而驀然醒覺，看清自己所犯的一切錯誤。

Often it takes some calamity to make us live in the present. Then suddenly we wake up and see all the mistakes we have made.

- 天才在自己的時代絕不會被理解。

  Genius is never understood in its own time.


- 我知道這個世界是不公平的，然而為何不會是一種有利於我的不公平？

  I know the world isn't fair, but why isn't it ever unfair in my favor?


- 讓你自己心無所繫，就是解決問題的上上策。

  Letting your mind play is the best way to solve problems.


- 生命有涯，無法做盡無謂之事。

  There is not enough time to do all the nothing we want to do.


- 週末不算是週末，除非你去做些毫無意義的事。

  Weekends don't count unless you spend them doing something completely pointless.


- 你憎恨的工作，才是真正的工作。

  A real job is a job you hate.


- 似乎人們一旦長大，就不懂什麼才叫酷。

  It seems like once people grow up, they have no idea what's cool.

# 戲劇界

# 柏格曼 (Ingmar Bergman, 1918-2007)

瑞典著名導演，其電影語彙大膽而前衛，被奉為當代電影大師。一生導演過62部電影，多數自行編劇，也導演超過170場的戲劇。每以簡約的影像風格、沉鬱的理性精神，探索人生各項問題，最為人所津津樂道的作品包括《第七封印》、《野草莓》、《處女之泉》、《魔鬼的眼睛》、《冬之光》、《假面》等。

● 影片如夢，如音樂，沒有藝術像影片那樣穿越我們的內心，直接訴諸我們的感情，深入靈魂的暗室。

Film as dream, film as music. No art passes our conscience in the way film does, and goes directly to our feelings, deep down into the dark rooms of our souls.

● 我靠直覺做一切決定，我把一枝矛擲入黑暗，那是直覺，然後我派一支軍隊進入黑暗尋找那枝矛，那就是才智。

I make all my decisions on intuition. I throw a spear into the darkness. That is intuition. Then I must send an army into the darkness to find the spear. That is intellect.

● 打從小時候開始，音樂一直是我尋求娛樂與刺激的一大源泉，我常以欣賞音樂的方式去體驗一部電影或戲劇。

Ever since childhood, music has been my great source of recreation and stimulation, and I often experience a film or play musically.

● 我年輕時，極端怕死，但現在卻認為那是非常、非常聰明的安排，一如燈滅，沒什麼好大驚小怪。

When I was young, I was extremely scared of dying. But now I think it a very, very wise arrangement. It's like a light that is extinguished. Not very much to make a fuss about.

- 我想我只拍過一部自己真正喜歡的片子，那就是《冬之光》，這部片子的分分秒秒無不依我所願。

  I think I have made just one picture that I really like, and that is "Winter Light". Everything is exactly as I wanted to have it, in every second of this picture.

- 劇院就像忠實的妻子，影片卻是一大冒險，也就是那位奢華、難纏的情婦。

  The theater is like a faithful wife. The film is the great adventure -- the costly, exacting mistress.

- 劇院是開始也是結束，實際上它就是一切，而電影院則屬於嫖妓與屠宰的行業。

  Theater is the beginning and end and actually everything, while cinema belongs to the whoring and slaughterhouse trade.

- 我對事物的基本觀點就是，不要對事物有任何基本觀點，我以前對人生極度武斷的看法，已漸消失無存。

  My basic view of things is - not to have any basic view of things. From having been exceedingly dogmatic, my views on life have gradually dissolved. They don't exist any longer.

- 我希望我永遠不會老到會去依賴宗教。

  I hope I never get so old I get religious.

# 卻爾登希斯頓 ( Charlton Heston, 1924-2008 )

美國著名的電影、電視演員，常飾演戰爭片裡的正面角色。代表作為《十誡》、《賓漢》、《鄧迪少校》、《超世紀諜殺案》等，因出演電影《賓漢》而獲得1959年第32屆奧斯卡最佳男主角獎。他是美國平民最高榮譽總統自由勳章的得主，晚年擔任美國步槍協會（NRA）主席。

● 我曾演過三次總統、三次聖人以及兩次天才，對任何人而言，恐怕都已夠了。

I've played three presidents, three saints and two geniuses - and that's probably enough for any man.

● 你有一生可過，若肯誠實面對自我，你的表現從未曾十全十美。

You can spend a lifetime, and, if you're honest with yourself, never once was your work perfect.

● 電影作為一種商業的困擾，就是它是一種藝術，而電影作為一種藝術的困擾，就是它是一種商業。

The trouble with movies as a business is that it's an art, and the trouble with movies as art is that it's a business.

● 我的信條就是，無所謂好槍或壞槍，一把槍在壞人手中，就是壞事，任何槍在好人手中，除了對壞人外，對誰都不構成威脅。

Here's my credo. There are no good guns, There are no bad guns. A gun in the hands of a bad man is a bad thing. Any gun in the hands of a good man is no threat to anyone, except bad people.

- 社會可以癒合它的傷口，印證於一切悲劇，那是百分之百的正確，印證於喜劇亦然，印證於歷史更是百試不爽。

  Society mends its wounds. And that's invariably true in all the tragedies, in the comedies as well. And certainly in the histories.

- 對一名演員而言，最大的損失莫過於失去其觀眾。

  For an actor, there is no greater loss than the loss of his audience.

- 政治正確，就是有禮的暴政。

  Political correctness is tyranny with manners.

- 人生是多麼美好的旅程，我分分秒秒都樂在其中。

  It's been quite a ride. I loved every minute of it.

- 演戲所給我的，就是有機會做許多其他的人。

  What acting offered me was the chance to be many other people.

- 我寧願演一名參議員，也不要當一名參議員。

  I'd rather play a senator than be one.

- 我有一張屬於另一世紀的臉孔。

  I have a face that belongs in another century.

# 保羅紐曼 (Paul Newman, 1925-2008)

美國影壇超級巨星、賽車手、慈善家，曾獲坎城影展、金球獎、艾美獎最佳演員獎，以及奧斯卡終身成就獎。一生演過60多部電影，包括《出埃及記》、《朱門巧婦》、《桃色風暴》、《虎豹小霸王》、《老千計狀元才》以及《刺激》等經典名片，前後榮獲9次奧斯卡提名，1986年並以《金錢本色》一片，奪得奧斯卡最佳男主角獎。

● 演戲其實並不是一種創意行業，而是一種詮釋行業。

Acting isn't really a creative profession. It's an interpretative one.

● 每次拿到一個劇本，我就會苦思自己該如何處理。我看到種種顏色、意象，它必須要有味道，一如墜入情網，無從解釋。

Every time I get a script it's a matter of trying to know what I could do with it. I see colors, imagery. It has to have a smell. It's like falling in love. You can't give a reason why.

● 如果你沒有敵人，就表示你沒有個性。

If you don't have enemies, you don't have character.

● 要是你在玩撲克，環顧牌桌，不知誰是凱子，那就是你了。

If you're playing a poker game and you look around the table and can't tell who the sucker is, it's you.

● 贏來的錢要比賺來的錢，倍感甜美。

Money won is twice as sweet as money earned.

- 人們維持婚姻，因為心甘情願，不是因為門已上鎖。

  People stay married because they want to, not because the doors are locked.

- 要做個演員，就須有赤子之心。

  To be an actor you have to be a child.

- 只有在孤獨時，你才會成長。

  You only grow when you are alone.

- 經營一種事業，規則有三，很幸運的，我們對其一無所知。

  There are three rules for running a business; fortunately, we don't know any of them.

- 誰能說誰是專家？

  Who's to say who's an expert?

- 我一直是一名性格演員。

  I was always a character actor.

# 高達 (Jean-Luc Godard, 1930- )

法國電影導演，新浪潮電影的代表人物。自50年代起，不斷在專業電影刊物如《電影筆記》發表影評，並開始從事電影創作至今。他能跳脫傳統電影語言，以創新的拍片技巧、實驗性的表現手法、跳躍式的剪輯，拍攝出具有高度批判性的影片，因而在電影史上佔有舉足輕重的地位。代表作有《狂人皮耶洛》、《巴黎，我愛你》等。

● 電影是世上最美的騙局。

Cinema is the most beautiful fraud in the world.

● 一部電影所需要的，充其量不過是一把槍和一個女人而已。

All you need for a movie is a gun and a girl.

● 電影不是一種拍攝人生的藝術，電影是某種介於藝術與人生的東西。不像繪畫與文學，電影既充實人生，同時也取材自人生，我努力將此一觀念呈現於自己的影片之中。文學與繪畫兩者自始即以藝術的面目存在，電影卻非如此。

The cinema is not an art which films life: the cinema is something between art and life. Unlike painting and literature, the cinema both gives to life and takes from it, and I try to render this concept in my films. Literature and painting both exist as art from the very start; the cinema doesn't.

● 對我而言，風格是內容的外在，內容是風格的裡子，就像一個人身體的內外，兩者一體，無法分割。

To me style is just the outside of content, and content the inside of style, like the outside and the inside of the human body. Both go together, they can't be separated.

- 我同情法國電影業，因為它沒錢；我同情美國電影業，因為它沒思想。

  I pity the French Cinema because it has no money. I pity the American Cinema because it has no ideas.


- 藝術吸引我們，只因為它洩露了我們最不為人知的自我。

  Art attracts us only by what it reveals of our most secret self.


- 一個故事應具有開頭、中間與結尾，但不一定非得按照那樣的次序。

  A story should have a beginning, a middle, and an end but not necessarily in that order.


- 我為打發時間而拍片。

  I make film to make time pass.


- 電影不是夢或幻想，它就是人生。

  Cinema is not a dream or a fantasy. It is life.


- 評論一部電影的最佳方法，就是去拍另一部。

  The best way to criticize a movie is to make another.

# 碧姬芭杜 ( Brigitte Bardot, 1934- )

法國演員、歌星、時裝模特兒、動物權運動份子, 右翼評論人。自1953至1973年, 計拍攝50多部電影, 因身材豐滿、作風大膽, 而有性感小野貓之稱,《上帝創造女人》是其從影的成名之作。1973年突然改變人生方向, 放棄影藝事業, 全心投入動物權益保護工作, 並成立基金會與流浪動物收容所。

- 某人外表上是明星, 實際上卻十分孤獨、疑神疑鬼。忍受此種心靈的孤獨, 是世上最苦之事。

  On the outside one is a star. But in reality, one is completely alone, doubting everything. To experience this loneliness of soul is the hardest thing in the world.

- 一張照片可以是生命中的吉光片羽, 為永恆留下見證, 它永不停歇地對你回顧。

  A photograph can be an instant of life captured for eternity that will never cease looking back at you.

- 每一種年齡都能迷人, 假如你能泰然處之的話。

  Every age can be enchanting, provided you live within it.

- 我把美麗與青春付與男人, 我將把智慧與經驗付與動物。

  I gave my beauty and my youth to men. I am going to give my wisdom and experience to animals.

- 寧可不忠實, 也不要不情願的忠實。

  It's better to be unfaithful than faithful without wanting to be.

- 他們也許會叫我罪人，但我問心無愧。

  They may call me a sinner, but I am at peace with myself.

- 人變老固然可悲，但變得成熟卻不錯。

  It is sad to grow old but nice to ripen.

- 人們永遠在找你的碴。

  People are forever finding something wrong with you.

- 做愛時我什麼都不想。

  I don't think when I make love.

- 女人愈想解放自己，就愈不快樂。

  Women get more unhappy the more they try to liberate themselves.

- 我喜歡戀愛，討厭分手，但我愛得自由，活得自由。

  I love to love and I hate to leave, but I love freely and I live freely.

# 茱莉安德魯斯 (Julie Andrews, 1935- )

英國女演員、歌手和作家。12歲開始在倫敦舞臺獻藝，
1954年轉往紐約發展，1956年領銜主演舞臺劇《窈窕淑
女》，該劇乃成為史上最受歡迎的歌舞劇之一。1964年，
主演電影《歡樂滿人間》，獲得奧斯卡最佳女演員獎，之
後主演電影《真善美》，聲名更如日中天。2007年，獲得
第13屆美國演員工會頒以「終身成就獎」的殊榮。

● 我是一個思想解放的女子，深信女人若做同等的事，就應領取
同等的酬勞，但我個人還是不脫女性本質，很樂意有可仰靠的
男性主管。

I am a liberated woman. And I do believe if a woman
does equal work she should be paid equal money. But
personally I am feminine and I do like male authority to
lean on.

● 所有愛情都會變調，我不曉得你是否能始終如一地全心去愛。

All love shifts and changes. I don't know if you can be
wholeheartedly in love all the time.

● 如果導演說你能演得更好，特別是在一場愛情戲中，那麼，就
令人感到十分尷尬了。

If the director says you can do better, particularly in a love
scene, then it is rather embarrassing.

● 李察波頓有一回打電話給我說，妳可知道妳是唯一從未跟我睡
過的女主角？我回答說，這樣子啊，請不要逢人就說，那可是
壞透的形象。

Richard Burton rang me up once and said, Do you know
you're my only leading lady I've never slept with? I said,
Well, please don't tell everybody, it's the worst image.

- 機會有時稍縱即逝；努力投入工作吧，準備好自己，當機會來臨，才能有所掌握。

  Sometimes opportunities float right past your nose. Work hard, apply yourself, and be ready. When an opportunity comes you can grab it.

- 有些人視紀律為眼中釘，對我而言，它卻是放我自由翱翔的一種命令。

  Some people regard discipline as a chore. For me, it is a kind of order that sets me free to fly.

- 所謂堅忍，就是失敗十九次，第二十次才成功。

  Perseverance is failing 19 times and succeeding the 20th.

- 我不是一個趕時髦的人，雖然我跟一般女人一樣喜歡衣服。

  I am not a trendy person, though I like clothes as much as the average woman.

- 講到化妝，我的看法是，做妳自己，讓妳自己受到注目；不要過度化妝，以致看不到真實的妳。

  When it comes to make-up, my message is, be yourself and let yourself be seen. Don't slosh so much make-up on that you can't see the real person.

- 面對攝影機的恐懼，依然如故。

  The thrill of being in front of a camera remains exactly the same.

# 伊莉莎白泰勒 ( Elizabeth Taylor, 1936- )

美國影壇巨星，有好萊塢的常青樹之稱。曾三度獲得奧斯卡獎提名，二次獲得奧斯卡最佳女演員獎，分別為1961年的《青樓豔妓》，以及1967年的《靈慾春宵》。近年投身慈善事業，致力於愛滋病的防治工作，在1991年並設立了伊莉莎白愛滋防治基金會。成名之作尚有《玉女神駒》、《埃及豔后》、《朱門巧婦》等。

- 要是我相信在報上所讀到有關我的種種八卦，我就有充分理由來恨我自己了。

  If I believed everything I read about myself in the press, I'd have good reason to hate myself.

- 同性戀者的創造力，已使這個城鎮在一切藝術領域實現諸多可能，除掉同性戀者，就沒有好萊塢。

  The creativity of homosexuals has made so much possible in this town, in all the arts! Take out the homosexuals and there's no Hollywood!

- 我只跟我下嫁的男人上床，有多少女人可以那樣主張？

  I've only slept with men I've been married to. How many women can make that claim?

- 當你涉入一樁醜聞，就會發現誰是你真正的朋友。

  You find out who your real friends are when you're involved in a scandal.

- 萬事都會讓我緊張，拍片除外。

  Everything makes me nervous - except making films.

- 我還沒讀過任何一本有關我自己的傳記。

  I haven't read any of the autobiographies about me.

- 我一向承認我是一個感情用事的人。

  I've always admitted that I'm ruled by my passions.

- 成功是一帖偉大的芳香劑，可除掉你過去一切的氣味。

  Success is a great deodorant. It takes away all your past smells.

- 我不認為布希總統在為愛滋病做任何事，事實上，我想他連愛滋一詞如何寫恐怕都搞不太清楚。

  I don't think President Bush is doing anything at all about Aids. In fact, I'm not sure he even knows how to spell Aids.

- 我希望我的墓碑上寫著：「她活過。」

  I want my tombstone to say "She Lived."

- 當人們說：「她要什麼有什麼」，我只有一個答案：「我尚未擁有明天」。

  When people say, "She's got everything," I've only one answer, "I haven't had tomorrow."

# 傑克尼克遜 ( Jack Nicholson, 1937- )

美國好萊塢巨星，先後獲得12次奧斯卡獎提名（8次男主角、4次男配角），其中1975年和1997年二次榮獲奧斯卡最佳男主角獎，1983年獲得奧斯卡最佳男配角獎。由於其傑出之演藝成就，1994年美國影藝學院特別頒以終身成就獎，第56屆金球獎亦授予終身成就獎。代表作有《逍遙騎士》、《飛越杜鵑窩》、《愛妳在心口難開》等。

- 我知道我能演，其他我會做的事卻屈指可數。

  I know I can act. There aren't too many other jobs I know how to do.

- 我不希望人們知道我實際的長相，這對演員不好。

  I don't want people to know what I'm actually like. It's not good for an actor.

- 世間只有兩種人你可以對他們說謊：警察與女友。

  There's only two people in your life you should lie to: the police and your girlfriend.

- 永遠不要給人忠告，因為對方不會言聽計從。

  Don't ever give anybody your best advice, because they're not going to follow it.

- 我們犯錯，稱之為「惡」；上帝犯錯，稱之為「自然」。

  When we make mistakes they call it evil. When God makes mistakes they call it Nature!

- 戴上太陽眼鏡，我是傑克尼克遜；不戴太陽眼鏡，我是六十歲的肥佬。

  With my sunglasses on, I'm Jack Nicholson. Without them, I'm fat and 60.

- 我的座右銘就是：要擁有更多美好時光。

  My motto is: more good times.

- 演戲是人人都中意的第二份工作。

  Acting is everybody's favorite second job.

- 我絕不會說我受一票我喜歡的演員之影響，因為我喜歡的演員千千萬萬，就某方面而言，我受他們全體的影響。

  I've never been able to say I've been influenced by a list of artists I like because I like thousands and thousands and I've been influenced in some way by all of them.

- 大部分演員早期的生涯，就是有什麼活計就幹什麼。

  Most of the early part of an actor's career, you do the jobs you get.

# 史蒂芬史匹柏 ( Steven Spielberg, 1947- )

美國著名電影導演、編劇和製片家，堪稱是當代最成功、最受推崇的影壇巨匠，以《搶救雷恩大兵》及《辛德勒的名單》兩度贏得奧斯卡最佳導演獎，此外《法櫃奇兵》、《魔宮傳奇》、《侏羅紀公園》、《紫色姊妹花》、《大白鯊》、《第三類接觸》等均是其票房席捲全球之作。

● 我要拍另一部電影，可以讓我們歡笑、落淚、感受世界的美好。我要做一些其他令我們開心的事兒。人生有時需要多開心一點，而為了那些生活不順心的人，好萊塢電影亦應有所行動。

I wanted to do another movie that could make us laugh and cry and feel good about the world. I wanted to do something else that could make us smile. This is a time when we need to smile more and Hollywood movies are supposed to do that for people in difficult times.

● 我這一生中特別值得驕傲的有三部電影，通常我不會透露我所拍過而令我滿意的影片名單……但有三部影片與我結緣很深，第一部是《ET》，第二部是《辛德勒的名單》，第三部是《搶救雷恩大兵》。

There are three movies that I am exceptionally proud of in my life, and I rarely commit to a list of films that I like, that I've made, ... but these are the three films that I was passionately connected to. The first was "ET," the second "Schindler's List," and third is "Saving Private Ryan."

● 我不喝咖啡，這一生中從未喝過咖啡，這部分的我恐怕是你們所不知道的。打從兒時起，我就一直討厭那種味道。

I don't drink coffee. I've never had a cup of coffee in my entire life; that's something you probably don't know about me. I've hated the taste since I was a kid.

- 人們已忘記如何講故事。故事不再有什麼中間或結局，通常它們會有一個開頭，永不休止的開頭。

  People have forgotten how to tell a story. Stories don't have a middle or an end any more. They usually have a beginning that never stops beginning.

- 大眾期待一切富於想像的東西，亦即任何盡可能發揮創意、遠離現實的東西。

  The public has an appetite for anything about imagination - anything that is as far away from reality as is creatively possible.

- 我們所有的人，在每一個年頭都是不一樣的人，我不認為我們終生都會一成不變。

  All of us every single year, we're a different person. I don't think we're the same person all our lives.

- 在電檢制度、良好品味與道德責任之間，還是有條界線可言。

  There is a fine line between censorship and good taste and moral responsibility.

- 年紀愈大，我就愈把電影看成是一種移動的奇蹟。

  The older I get, the more I look at movies as a moving miracle.

- 為什麼要花一塊錢來買書籤？為什麼不就用一塊錢來當書籤？

  Why pay a dollar for a bookmark? Why not use the dollar for a bookmark?

# 妮可基嫚 ( Nicole Kidman, 1967- )

澳洲籍美國巨星，2001年以《紅磨坊》一片獲得奧斯卡提名，2003年在《時時刻刻》一片中以精湛之演技，一口氣奪下了金球獎影后、英國影藝學院影后，以及第75屆奧斯卡最佳女主角獎。她長期熱心參與慈善工作，從1994年起，就擔任「聯合國兒童基金會」親善大使，2004年並因此獲得聯合國頒予「世界公民」之榮銜。

● 我認為，每一個角色都會有一點你的影子，而且會如影隨形般跟隨你一輩子，我不認為你會把其中任何一個拋諸腦後。

I think each role takes a little from you and circles around you for the rest of your life. I don't think you ever abandon any of them.

● 我所扮演的種種不同角色，都變成我生命中的所愛。

These different people that I play become the loves of my life.

● 不論你這一生做什麼，千萬不要放棄自己的夢想。

Whatever you do in life, don't give up on your own dreams.

● 如果你進入生命的陰暗面，一旦穿越過它，就會展現更多力量與熱情。

If you enter the dark side of life, and come through it, you emerge with more strength and passion.

● 一天天的向前邁進，保持微笑，要記住明天又是另外一天。

Move forward one day at a time, keep smiling, and remember that tomorrow is another day.

- 戀愛是一件很勇敢的事，你非得心甘情願的全然信任另外一個人不可，那是非常不容易、真正不容易、十分勇敢的。

  It's a very brave thing to fall in love. You have to be willing to trust somebody else with your whole being, and that's very difficult, really difficult and very brave.

- 工作的力量，以及創意的力量，可以成為你的救贖。

  The power of work, and the power of creativity, can be your salvation.

- 要過一個真正圓滿的人生，就須敞開心胸。

  To live a really full life, you must stay open.

- 我喜歡演戲，但帶孩子們去動物園卻更好玩。

  I love acting, but it's much more fun taking the kids to the zoo.

- 要想性感，不一定非得裸露。

  You don't have to be naked to be sexy.

- 在美國，除非你上電視，否則一定沒沒無聞。

  You're not anyone in America unless you're on TV.

# 企管界

# 馬登 ( Orison Swett Marden, 1850-1924 )

美國當代最偉大的激勵大師、積極思想導師及心靈演說家，也是美國著名雜誌《成功》的創辦人，被公認為美國現代成功學研究的奠基人。所著勵志書籍眾多，極力主張人生要從心靈的困頓中解放出來，超越平庸。著作被譯成20餘種語言銷行全球，著有《像贏家一樣思考》、《成功需要成長與創新》、《喚醒內心的巨人》、《沒有藉口》、《一生的資本》等。

- 不要等待特殊的機會，而要把握尋常的時機，使其變成良機；弱者等待機會，強者創造機會。

  Don't wait for extraordinary opportunities. Seize common occasions and make them great. Weak men wait for opportunities; strong men make them.

- 所有成大事者，都懷有遠大夢想。

  All men who have achieved great things have been great dreamers.

- 森林、湖泊、河流、雲與風、星辰與花朵、巨大的冰河與晶瑩的雪花，凡此種種有生命或無生命的存在形式，都在人類的靈魂上留下印記。

  Forests, lakes, and rivers, clouds and winds, stars and flowers, stupendous glaciers and crystal snowflakes - every form of animate or inanimate existence, leaves its impress upon the soul of man.

- 樂觀的人在別人看到失敗處，看到成功；在別人看到陰影與暴風雨處，看到陽光。

  The hopeful man sees success where others see failure, sunshine where others see shadows and storm.

- 你所尋覓的黃金機會，就繫於你自身，它並不在於你的環境，不在於運氣或機會，抑或他人的臂助，而就只繫於你一己之身。

  The golden opportunity you are seeking is in yourself. It is not in your environment; it is not in luck or chance, or the help of others; it is in yourself alone.

- 有影響力的人，就是成功的人，不論其窮富。

  The influential man is the successful man, whether he be rich or poor.

- 喜悅使心靈與容貌年輕；暢快的一笑，使我們跟自己交好，也與周遭每一個人交好。

  Joyfulness keeps the heart and face young. A good laugh makes us better friends with ourselves and everybody around us.

- 阮囊羞澀者是窮人，但除了錢之外別無長物者，是更窮的人，唯有不靠擁有財物而能享受生活的人，才是富人；貪得無厭者，縱有萬貫家私，仍屬窮人。

  The man who has no money is poor, but one who has nothing but money is poorer. He only is rich who can enjoy without owning; he is poor who though he has millions is covetous.

- 只要盡力而為，就不算是失敗之人。

  No man fails who does his best.

# 富比士 ( Bertie Charles Forbes , 1880-1954 )

美國傳播媒體鉅子。出生於蘇格蘭，1901年在南非約翰尼斯堡創辦《蘭德每日郵報》，1904年移民美國，最初擔任財經雜誌編輯，並出任赫斯特報系專欄作家。1917年在紐約創辦《富比士》雜誌，其家族開始崛起。著有《打造美國的人》、《美國的火車巨人》、《如何賺取最多的商業利益》等。

- 一個已竭盡其力，而且也自知已盡力的人，就是成功者，縱然在世人心目中會把他當成失敗者看待。

  The man who has done his level best, and who is conscious that he has done his best, is a success, even though the world may write him down as a failure.

- 成大事者，無懼於致力大事，也無懼於冒險圖成。

  The men who have done big things are those who were not afraid to attempt big things, who were not afraid to risk failure in order to gain success.

- 我們的前途與命運，仰靠我們的意志多過於仰靠我們的雙手，因為雙手只不過是意志的工具罷了。

  Our future and our fate lie in our wills more than in our hands, for our hands are but the instruments of our wills.

- 做一個一流的貨車司機，要比做一個不入流的經理，更有光彩與成就感。

  There is more credit and satisfaction in being a first-rate truck driver than a tenth-rate executive.

- 工作是人生的主菜，享樂只是甜點而已。

  Work is the meat of life, pleasure the dessert.

- 真正的財富，是內心所擁有的財富。

  Real riches are the riches possessed inside.

- 打沒有沙坑與障礙的高爾夫球，既乏味又單調，人生亦復如此。

  Golf without bunkers and hazards would be tame and monotonous. So would life.

- 牢記舉頭三尺有神明的人，最不會發怒。

  He best keeps from anger who remembers that God is always looking upon him.

- 真正的朋友可以分擔我們的愁苦，倍增我們的喜樂。

  The real friend is he or she who can share all our sorrow and double our joys.

- 平庸的人等待機會上門，堅強、能幹、機警的人尋覓機會。

  Mediocre men wait for opportunity to come to them. Strong, able, alert men go after opportunity.

# 拿破崙希爾 （Napoleon Hill, 1883-1970）

現代成功學奠基人，世界上最偉大的勵志大師之一，也是成功學、人際關係學的培訓大師。擔任過美國威爾遜總統及羅斯福總統的顧問。曾花費二十年時光，訪問五百多位美國成功人士，以探求成功的訣竅。最有名的著作《思考致富》（Think and Grow Rich），暢銷全球，被譯成20多種文字，其他名著尚有《人人都能成功》、《成功規律》等。

- 要珍惜你的憧憬與夢想，因為它們是你的靈魂之子，是你最終成就的藍圖。

  Cherish your visions and your dreams as they are the children of your soul, the blueprints of your ultimate achievements.

- 渴望是所有成就的起點，它不是期盼，不是願望，而是一種凌駕一切的熊熊欲念。

  Desire is the starting point of all achievement, not a hope, not a wish, but a keen pulsating desire which transcends everything.

- 偉大的成就往往出於重大犧牲，絕不是出於自私自利的結果。

  Great achievement is usually born of great sacrifice, and is never the result of selfishness.

- 如果你非講別人的壞話不可，不要用說的，而去寫在水邊的沙上。

  If you must speak ill of another, do not speak it, write it in the sand near the water's edge.

- 機會，經常以災禍或一時挫敗的形式出現。

  Opportunity often comes disguised in the form of misfortune, or temporary defeat.

- 向別人推銷自己的上上之策，就是先向自己推銷別人。

  The best way to sell yourself to others is first to sell the others to yourself.

- 開口前要三思，因為你的言辭與影響，會在別人心中種下成功或失敗的種子。

  Think twice before you speak, because your words and influence will plant the seed of either success or failure in the mind of another.

- 從人類思想中所挖掘出的黃金，要多過從地上所挖出的。

  More gold has been mined from the thoughts of men than has been taken from the earth.

- 所謂目標，就是訂有期限的夢想。

  A goal is a dream with a deadline.

- 愛迪生在發明電燈前，失敗了一萬次，如果你失敗個幾回，千萬不可氣餒。

  Edison failed 10, 000 times before he made the electric light. Do not be discouraged if you fail a few times.

# 克萊門史東（W. Clement Stone, 1902-2002）

美國聯合保險公司創辦人、成功學大師、勵志書作家。20歲時開始獨立創業，30出頭就成為商業鉅子，到1979年，所創立的保險公司已擁有超過10億美元的資產。作為成功致富的導師，曾編著諸多成功學書籍，還創辦有月刊《成功無限》（Success Unlimited），鼓勵世人以積極的人生態度邁向致富之路。著有自傳《永不失敗的成功制度》。

● 人與人之間差異很小，但那種小小的差異會造成大大的不同。小小的差異就是態度，而大大的不同就在於態度是正面抑或負面。

There is little difference in people, but that little difference makes a big difference. The little difference is attitude. The big difference is whether it is positive or negative.

● 選擇朋友要小心，因為你會變得像他們。

Be careful the friends you choose for you will become like them.

● 要有勇氣說「不」，要有勇氣面對真相，要為所當為，這些都是正直過活的萬靈鑰匙。

Have the courage to say no. Have the courage to face the truth. Do the right thing because it is right. These are the magic keys to living your life with integrity.

● 要想快樂，就要使他人快樂。

To be happy, make other people happy.

● 要以月亮為目標，就算未射中，也會射中星星。

Aim for the moon. If you miss, you may hit a star.

- 努力、努力、努力，不斷努力是成為任何專家的不二法門。

  Try, try, try, and keep on trying is the rule that must be followed to become an expert in anything.

- 每一不利，就有相對應的利益。

  To every disadvantage there is a corresponding advantage.

- 每一個偉人、每一個成功的人，不管致力於什麼行業，都瞭解這句話的妙用：每一逆境，都存有對等或更大利益的種子。

  Every great man, every successful man, no matter what the field of endeavor, has known the magic that lies in these words: every adversity has the seed of an equivalent or greater benefit.

- 我們有個麻煩，「恭喜」，但它很棘手，「那麼加倍恭喜」。

  We have a problem. "Congratulations." But it's a tough problem. "Then double congratulations."

- 不管你是誰或你做過什麼，你總可以成為你想做的那種人。

  Regardless of who you are or what you have been, you can be what you want to be.

# 鄧普頓 (John Templeton, 1912-2008)

美國金融投資大師，在1999年被《Money》雜誌選為「20世紀最偉大的操盤手」。當市場仍侷限於美國華爾街投資時，鄧氏獨具慧眼，創立第一檔全球股票基金，成為全球化投資的先河。他的投資哲學就是不要盲目追隨群眾，而應逆勢操作。他自1987年退休之後，全心投入傳教事業，並著書立說，闡釋其人生理念。

- 要投資在最悲觀的時刻。

  Invest at the point of maximum pessimism.

- 務必分散你的投資。

  Diversify your investments.

- 最悲觀的時候，就是下場買進的最佳時機，也就是最樂觀的時候。

  The time of maximum pessimism is the best time to buy and the time of maximum optimism.

- 如果你想比大眾有更好的表現，那就必須做跟大眾不一樣的事。

  If you want to have a better performance than the crowd, you must do things differently from the crowd.

- 要想在市場上真正獲得成功，你得揚棄以技術分析作為投資的方法，而做一個基本面的信徒。

  Rejecting technical analysis as a method for investing, you must be a fundamentalist to be really successful in the market.

- 所謂個人能找到神的這種觀念，是非常自我中心的，就好像浪花以為它能找到大海一樣。

  The idea that an individual can find God is terribly self-centered. It is like a wave thinking it can find the sea.


- 在投資上最危險的四個字，就是「這回不同」。

  The four most dangerous words in investing are "This time it's different."


- 讓我們敬拜上帝，但要曉得，我們所敬拜的上帝，是超越自己所能理解的。

  Let's worship Divinity, but understand the Divinity we worship is beyond our comprehension.


- 我想到人生只能走這麼一趟，而且時間不長，那麼此生究竟要何去何從才能嘉惠世世代代？

  I thought, I'm only going to be on this planet once, and only for a short time. What can I do with my life that will lead to permanent benefits?


- 如今我聚焦於精神的財富，比以前的我更忙碌、更熱心、更快活。

  I focus on spiritual wealth now, and I'm busier, more enthusiastic, and more joyful than I have ever been.

# 巴菲特（Warren Buffett, 1930- ）

美國有史以來最偉大的投資家、企業家、慈善家，他倡導的價值投資理論，舉世風靡。巴氏天生具有投資才華，11歲時就購買了生平第一張股票。他憑著對股票、外匯市場精準的操作，積聚龐大財富，並以620億美元的身價，擠下長期排名居首的微軟創辦人比爾蓋茲，成為為世界首富。2007年，獲選《時代》雜誌全球百大最具影響力人士之一。

● 把門關上，我要教你發財之道：在別人貪心的時候，你要擔心，但在別人擔心的時候，你要貪心。

I will tell you how to become rich. Close the doors. Be fearful when others are greedy. Be greedy when others are fearful.

● 在人人都熱中於股票的時候，大多數人也都會興致勃勃，而真正應對股票感興趣的時候，應是無人加以一顧之時，你不可能靠買熱門東西而發財。

Most people get interested in stocks when everyone else is. The time to get interested is when no one else is. You can't buy what is popular and do well.

● 不少成功，可歸因於按兵不動，多數投資人都無法抵擋不斷買進賣出的誘惑。

Much success can be attributed to inactivity. Most investors cannot resist the temptation to constantly buy and sell.

● 時間，是爛企業的敵人，卻是好企業的朋友。

Time is the enemy of the poor business and the friend of the great business.

- 花二十年才能建立的名聲，五分鐘就能毀掉，一念及此，你就會有不同的作為。

  It takes 20 years to build a reputation and five minutes to ruin it. If you think about that, you'll do things differently.

- 如果你對擁有某樣東西十年之久，惴惴難安，那麼就連擁有它十分鐘都可不必了。

  If you don't feel comfortable owning something for 10 years, then don't own it for 10 minutes.

- 你若不認識珠寶，就一定要認識珠寶商。

  If you don't know jewelry, know the jeweler.

- 今日有人可以坐在樹蔭下，是因為有人很久以前種下一棵樹。

  Someone's sitting in the shade today because someone planted a tree a long time ago.

- 不要擔心股票市場如何，要把焦點放在公司的表現如何。

  Don't worry about what the stock market will do, focus on what the company will do.

- 如果一家企業做得好，其股票終究會跟上來。

  If a business does well, the stock eventually follows.

# 羅勃特清崎 (Robert Kiyosaki, 1947- )

全球暢銷書《富爸爸、窮爸爸》（Rich Dad, Poor Dad）作者，也是一位投資家、專精於礦業和房地產的企業家，同時也是一名教育家。1985年，與友人合作創辦國際教育公司，主持各種商業投資課程，並曾主持電視節目。其暢銷書尚有：《富爸爸大預言》、《富爸爸商學院》、《富爸爸成功的故事》、《富爸爸辭職創業前的10堂課》等。

● 你的成就如何，可用你欲望的強度、你夢想的大小，以及你一向怎樣處理挫折，來加以衡量。

The size of your success is measured by the strength of your desire; the size of your dream; and how you handle disappointment along the way.

● 大人物有大夢想，小人物有小夢想。假如你想改變自己，那就要從改變自己夢想的規模來開始。

Big people have big dreams and small people have small dreams. If you want to change who you are, begin by changing the size of your dreams.

● 你要懂得資產與負債的差別，資產是把錢放進你的荷包，而負債則是從你的荷包中取錢。有錢人瞭解其差異，故買資產，不買負債。

You need to understand the difference between an asset and a liability. An asset puts money in your pocket and a liability takes money from your pocket. The rich understand the difference and buy assets, not liabilities.

● 窮人與中產階級為錢工作，富人讓錢為其工作。

The poor and middle class work for money. The rich have money work for them.

- 多數投資客說「不要冒險」，有錢的投資客卻不惜冒險。

  Most investors say "Don't take risks." The rich investor takes risks.

- 富人與窮人之間的唯一差別，就是如何利用時間。

  The only difference between a rich person and poor person is how they use their time.

- 「今日」是贏家的用語，「明日」是輸家的用語。

  Today is the word for winners and tomorrow is the word for losers.

- 明日只存在於夢想家與失敗者的心目中。

  Tomorrows only exist in the minds of dreamers and losers.

- 每一項麻煩的內部，都存在著一個機會。

  Inside of every problem lies an opportunity.

- 記住，你的心靈是你最大的資產，要放入什麼東西一定得小心。

  Remember, your mind is your greatest asset, so be careful what you put into it.

# 音樂界

# 馬勒 (Gustav Mahler, 1860-1911)

奧地利的猶太裔作曲家與指揮家,是浪漫時期後期最偉大的交響樂作曲家之一,被視作連接19世紀與現代音樂的大師級音樂家。一生總共創作十首交響曲,20世紀樂壇的樂風及創作技巧深受其影響。1897年擔任維也納劇院的指揮,1909-1910年出任紐約交響樂團指揮,代表作有交響樂《巨人》、《復活》和《大地之歌》等。

● 如果一個作曲家能夠用言語表達出他所要說的,他就用不著多此一舉地用音樂去表達了。

If a composer could say what he had to say in words he would not bother trying to say it in music.

● 問題不只在於征服一個前所未知的山峰,而也在於一步步地探索出一條攻頂的新路。

It's not just a question of conquering a summit previously unknown, but of tracing, step by step, a new pathway to it.

● 絕不要被同時代人的意見左右,要繼續穩健地走自己的路。

Never let oneself be guided by the opinion of one's contemporaries. Continue steadfastly on one's way.

● 要是你認為你讓聽眾感到厭煩,那就要演奏得慢一點,而非加快速度。

If you think you're boring your audience, go slower not faster.

● 演奏短曲較容易達到理想的效果。

It is easier to achieve a desired result in short pieces.

- 作曲時我所期望的以及我所想像的，不一定都能付諸實現。

  What I wanted and what I visualized while composing has not always been realized.

- 訓練、工作。工作、訓練。

  Discipline, work. Work, discipline.

- 幸運的是，總有一些東西仍待收穫，因此我們絕不可懶散下來。

  Fortunately, something always remains to be harvested. So let us not be idle.

- 你必須揚棄一切膚淺、一切慣例、一切虛浮與幻想。

  You must renounce all superficiality, all convention, all vanity and delusion.

- 在初期，音樂只是室內樂，意指在一個小空間裡讓一小群聽眾欣賞。

  In its beginnings, music was merely chamber music, meant to be listened to in a small space by a small audience.

# 史特拉汶斯基（Igor Stravinsky, 1882-1971）

美籍俄裔作曲家，是20世紀最具影響的作曲家之一，也是西方現代音樂的代表人物。其創作風格多變，革新過三個不同的音樂流派：原始主義、新古典主義以及序列主義，被人們譽為是音樂界中的畢卡索。1913年的《春之祭》是其一生音樂創作的代表作，也確立了其樂壇地位。後期作品有《阿貢》、《哀歌》、《樂章》和《安魂曲》等。

● 指揮一職主要是為「浪漫」音樂而設，「古典」音樂消除了指揮，我們不記得他在裡面所扮演的角色。

Conductors' careers are made for the most part with "Romantic" music. "Classic" music eliminates the conductor; we do not remember him in it.

● 教堂懂得聖歌作者所懂得的：音樂禮讚上帝，音樂比教堂建築及其所有的裝飾，更能禮讚上帝；它是教堂最了不起的門面。

The Church knew what the psalmist knew: Music praises God. Music is well or better able to praise him than the building of the church and all its decoration; it is the Church's greatest ornament.

● 真正的作曲家，時時刻刻都在思考著自己的作品，對此他不會一直意識得到，但後來當他驚覺應何去何從時，他才有所明白。

The real composer thinks about his work the whole time; he is not always conscious of this, but he is aware of it later when he suddenly knows what he will do.

● 要想創作，就必須有股衝勁，而什麼東西會比愛情更具力道？

In order to create there must be a dynamic force, and what force is more potent than love?

- 大體說來，音樂欣賞的問題就在於，人們理應被教成愛好音樂，卻被教成對音樂太過尊敬。

  The trouble with music appreciation in general is that people are taught to have too much respect for music they should be taught to love it instead.

- 次等的藝術家借用，偉大的藝術家偷取。

  Lesser artists borrow, great artists steal.

- 我的音樂最能被兒童與動物理解。

  My music is best understood by children and animals.

- 傾聽是一種努力，僅僅去聽卻沒啥價值，鴨子也會聽。

  To listen is an effort, and just to hear is no merit. A duck hears also.

- 我是一名音樂發明家。

  I am an inventor of music.

- 罪惡不能一筆勾消，只能被寬恕。

  Sins cannot be undone, only forgiven.

# 魯賓斯坦 (Arthur Rubinstein, 1887-1982)

美籍波蘭鋼琴家。以演奏蕭邦、德布西、舒曼和布拉姆斯等音樂家的作品見長，公認是20世紀最偉大的蕭邦詮釋者。自幼習琴，13歲時就和柏林愛樂合作演奏莫札特第23號鋼琴協奏曲，一生演奏生涯逾80載，堪稱鋼琴界的長青樹。晚年寫有自傳3卷，分別敘述其青年、中年和晚年的演奏生涯。

- 我感受得到那種公眾與我之間的暗通款曲，我能用空中的一個小小音符拉住他們，使他們屏息以待，那可是妙不可言的一刻。

  I feel that special secret current between the public and me. I can hold them with one little note in the air, and they will not breathe. That is a great, great moment.

- 能活著、能看、能走，能擁有房子、音樂、繪畫，在在都是奇蹟，我已經掌握住不斷體現奇蹟的生活技巧。

  To be alive, to be able to see, to walk, to have houses, music, paintings - it's all a miracle. I have adopted the technique of living life miracle to miracle.

- 人生是非得參與的比賽，好友，這是我們起碼所瞭解的真理，因而要樂活起來，不要隨著重重魅影的出沒而沮喪。

  Life is the game that must be played, this truth at least, good friends, we know; so live and laugh, nor be dismayed as one by one the phantoms go.

- 當然，成功別無公式可言，或許只有無條件的接受人生以及人生所帶來的一切。

  Of course there is no formula for success except perhaps an unconditional acceptance of life and what it brings.

- 有時在我坐下練琴時，室中別無一人，我必須壓抑住去按鈴找電梯生，付錢請他進來聽琴的衝動。

  Sometimes when I sit down to practice and there is no one else in the room, I have to stifle an impulse to ring for the elevator man and offer him money to come in and hear me.

- 向一位年輕貌美的女子求婚，要很有勇氣，請相信我，用鋼琴彈整本彼德洛希卡，卻要容易得多。

  It took great courage to ask a beautiful young woman to marry me. Believe me, it is easier to play the whole Petrushka on the piano.

- 我已領悟，你若熱愛生活，生活也會以愛還報。

  I have found that if you love life, life will love you back.

- 就算是在我生病沮喪之時，我依然熱愛生命。

  Even when I'm sick and depressed, I love life.

- 大部分的人以條件來求取快樂，但快樂只能在不設定任何條件情形下，被人感知。

  Most people ask for happiness on condition. Happiness can only be felt if you don't set any condition.

# 路易斯阿姆斯壯 ( Louis Armstrong, 1901-1971 )

美國最具影響力的爵士歌手、小號演奏家，也是首位將單一樂器從以往集體演奏的傳統中解放出來的重要推手，有「爵士樂之父」的稱號。他以渾厚沙啞的嗓音、親切溫暖的演唱方式，贏得舉世樂迷的青睞，並樹立其在流行樂壇屹立不搖的地位。1949年二月登上美國《時代雜誌》封面，是該刊有史以來以爵士樂手作為封面報導的第一人。

● 作為「熱門音樂」的愛好者與演奏者，我曾被問過千百次「熱門音樂」是否會消失，我總是說一定不會。

As a lover of "Hot Music" as well as a player, I have been asked hundreds of times if I thought "Hot Music" would die out. I said no indeed.

● 音樂若不能提供給大眾欣賞的話，就一文不值，要緊的是要為聽眾而活，因為你之所以上場，就是為了娛樂眾人。

The music ain't worth nothing if you can't lay it on the public. The main thing is to live for that audience, 'cause what you're there for is to please the people.

● 我全部的生命、全部的靈魂、全部的精神，就是用來吹奏小號。

My whole life, my whole soul, my whole spirit is to blow that horn.

● 對一名爵士樂手而言，記憶中的陳年往事何其重要。

The memory of things gone is important to a jazz musician.

● 所有的音樂都是民俗音樂，我從未聽過一匹馬唱歌。

All music is folk music. I ain't never heard a horse sing a song.

- 我們所演奏的，就是人生。

  What we play is life.

- 絕不要用同樣的方式演奏兩次。

  Never play a thing the same way twice.

- 世上有兩種音樂，好音樂與爛音樂，我只演奏好的那種。

  There is two kinds of music, the good, and the bad. I play the good kind.

- 要不是有爵士樂，就不會有搖滾樂。

  If it hadn't been for Jazz, there wouldn't be no rock and roll.

- 我不讓我的嘴巴說出自己腦袋所不能忍受的話語。

  I don't let my mouth say nothin' my head can't stand.

- 音樂家無所謂退休，他們心中不再有音樂時，他們才會停歇。

  Musicians don't retire; they stop when there's no more music in them.

# 彼得森 (Oscar Peterson, 1925-2007)

加拿大爵士樂鋼琴家和歌唱家。出身音樂家庭，七歲習琴，高中時代，即獲得蒙特婁當地電臺的表演合約，1949年在美國卡耐基音樂廳初次登場，聲名鵲起。他受現代爵士樂的影響，發展出自己個人獨特演奏風格，而成為爵士鋼琴中的領袖級人物，也是業界灌錄唱片最多的樂師之一。最為人熟知的專輯有《在音樂會上》、《一位藝術家的歷史》等經典之作。

● 我憑著我的感覺彈奏。

I play as I feel.

● 你不僅要懂得你自己的樂器，也必須懂得他人的樂器，以及如何隨時給予支援，那就是爵士樂。

You not only have to know your own instrument, you must know the others and how to back them up at all times. That's jazz.

● 有些人喜歡把他們心目中的爵士樂，搞得很哲學、很玄，你不需要什麼開場白，彈奏就是了。

Some people try to get very philosophical and cerebral about what they're trying to say with jazz. You don't need any prologues, you just play.

● 音樂界是第一個打破種族藩籬的，因為要一起表演，就必須喜歡跟你合作的人，如果心中有任何種族上的顧慮，就無法做到。

The music field was the first to break down racial barriers, because in order to play together, you have to love the people you are playing with, and if you have any racial inhibitions, you wouldn't be able to do that.

- 太多的爵士鋼琴家把自己侷限於一種個人的風格，也就是所謂的商標。他們把自己限制在一種形式的演奏。

  Too many jazz pianists limit themselves to a personal style, a trademark, so to speak. They confine themselves to one type of playing.

- 重要的是合奏的聲音，即使你是在獨奏也一樣。

  It's the group sound that's important, even when you're playing a solo.

- 如果你有任何有價值的東西要表達，人們就會傾聽。

  If you have something to say of any worth then people will listen to you.

- 我不會因為我認為它會賣上三千萬張才去錄製，我不會掉以輕心，賣一張，就是一張。

  I don't do something because I think it will sell 30 million albums. I couldn't care less. If it sells one, it sells one.

- 我相信用整架鋼琴作為唯一的樂器，也能表達可能呈現的種種音樂理念。

  I believe in using the entire piano as a single instrument capable of expressing every possible musical idea.

# 戴維斯 (Miles Davis, 1926-1991)

美國爵士樂小號手、樂隊領隊和作曲家。是爵士樂史上最重要的人物,二次世界大戰以後,每一次爵士樂的重大變革,戴維斯都是扮演前鋒角色,因而被尊稱為爵士樂永遠的教父。其作品中最常被人演出的有《午夜時分》、《納迪斯》、《里程碑》、《太陽能》與《那又如何》等。

● 我念茲在茲的就是創作,我的未來開始於每天早上醒來之時⋯⋯每天我都可以找到某些跟我生活有關的創意。

I'm always thinking about creating. My future starts when I wake up every morning... Every day I find something creative to do with my life.

● 有時你必須演奏很長的時間,才能演奏得像自己。

Sometimes you have to play a long time to be able to play like yourself.

● 不要演奏樂譜上有的東西,要演奏樂譜上沒有的東西。

Don't play what's there, play what's not there.

● 對我而言,音樂與生活全都與風格息息相關。

For me, music and life are all about style.

● 創造力與才華跟年紀無關,你有就有,沒有就沒有,年齡的增長無助於此。

Creativity and genius don't know nothing about age; either you got it or you don't, and being old is not going to help you get it.

- 不必懼怕錯誤，沒有什麼錯誤可言。

  Do not fear mistakes. There are none.

- 首先你模仿，然後再創新。

  First you imitate, then you innovate.

- 你若為了某個女人、某個男人、某種膚色或某些財富，而犧牲了你的藝術，那麼，你也就難以指望了。

  If you sacrifice your art because of some woman, or some man, or some colour, or for some wealth, you can't be trusted.

- 美國人不喜歡任何形式的藝術，老兄，他們一心一意所追求的，就是賺錢而已。

  Americans don't like any form of art, man. All they like to do is make money.

- 沒有了音樂，人生將是一場錯誤。

  Without music, life would be a mistake.

# 帕華洛帝 (Luciano Pavarotti, 1935-2007)

義大利歌劇抒情男高音演唱家，為當代最受歡迎的男高音之一，被公認是20世紀最傑出的美聲唱法歌劇演唱家，以能充分掌握高音音域而舉世聞名。成名之後經常在世界各地巡演，有時獨唱，有時則和多明哥與卡列拉斯同台獻藝，三人並稱為「世界三大男高音」。一生獲獎無數，包括5座葛萊美獎和2001年的甘迺迪中心榮譽獎。

- 我終究是一名歌劇演唱家，人們會這樣紀念著我。

  Above all, I am an opera singer. This is how people will remember me.

- 擁有較好的聲音，並不表示就能做較好的歌手。

  The better voice doesn't mean being a better singer.

- 專注是一切，在我要演出的那一天，任何人跟我講什麼，我都充耳不聞。

  Concentration is everything. On the day I'm performing, I don't hear anything anyone says to me.

- 我們是跟自己競爭，我盡可能有更好的表現，我是跟自己搏鬥，而非跟他人交手。

  The rivalry is with ourselves. I try to be better than is possible. I fight against myself, not against the other.

- 對我而言，人生快事莫過於音樂製作了，那是任何情感的絕佳呈現。

  For me, music making is the most joyful activity possible, the most perfect expression of any emotion.

- 我是一名完美主義者，就算已表現得差強人意，我總認為我還可以表現得更好。

  I'm a perfectionist, and I always think that I can do better what I have done, even if it's good.


- 兒童若未在早年引入音樂之門，我相信他們身上某些基本的東西實際上已被剝奪。

  If children are not introduced to music at an early age, I believe something fundamental is actually being taken from them.


- 我怕高音嗎？當然我怕，有什麼正常人不怕呢？

  Am I afraid of high notes? Of course I am afraid. What sane man is not?


- 在我們這個行業，沒有什麼奇才，你若檢視過去所有偉大的演唱家，沒有人稱得上是奇才。

  There is no prodigy in our profession. If you see all the great singer of the past, none of them are.


- 人們認為我訓練有素，那不是訓練，而是敬業，兩者大不相同。

  People think I am disciplined. It is not discipline. It is devotion. There is a great difference.

# 巴布狄倫 (Bob Dylan, 1941- )

美國搖滾樂傳奇歌手與作曲家，其歌曲在1960年代成為當代之音。所寫的歌以民謠傳統為基調，其中《隨風飛揚》和《正在改變的時代》，成為民權運動之歌。他以嘶啞的嗓音唱出個人對時代的批判，唱紅的歌曲有《納什維爾地平線》，《重訪61號公路》、《金髮人論金髮人》、《軌道上的血跡》、《慾望》、《異教徒》等。

● 受人注目會是一種負擔，耶穌就因為惹人側目而被釘十字架，所以我常消失無蹤。

Being noticed can be a burden. Jesus got himself crucified because he got himself noticed. So I disappear a lot.

● 沒有人是自由的，連鳥兒都難免被禁錮在天空。

No one is free, even the birds are chained to the sky.

● 要珍惜你所有的記憶，因為你無法再活一回。

Take care of all your memories. For you cannot relive them.

● 所謂歌曲，就是那種會自行走透透的東西。

A song is anything that can walk by itself.

● 樂迷有什麼用？你不能把掌聲當早餐，也不能帶著掌聲入夢。

What good are fans? You can't eat applause for breakfast. You can't sleep with it.

● 我所可以做的，就是做自己，不管那是什麼樣的我。

All I can do is be me, whoever that is.

- 我為芸芸大眾發聲，我是一個世代的發言人。

  I'm speaking for all of us. I'm the spokesman for a generation.

- 要活在法律管不到的地方，就非得誠實不可。

  To live outside the law, you must be honest.

- 如果你需要一個能信得過的人，那就信任你自己好了。

  If you need somebody you can trust, trust yourself.

- 就因你喜歡我的作品，不代表我欠你什麼。

  Just because you like my stuff doesn't mean I owe you anything.

- 每種享樂都有其痛苦的一面，你得付出代價，而且無怨無悔。

  Every pleasures got an edge of pain, pay for your ticket and don't complain.

# 賽門 ( Paul Simon, 1941- )

美國作曲家、歌唱家和吉他手,為舉世風靡的二重唱「賽門與葛芬柯」的一員,曾唱紅無數家喻戶曉的歌曲,如《惡水上的大橋》、《寂靜之聲》、《羅賓遜太太》等等。係美國國會圖書館「蓋西文獎」首屆獲獎人,90年代入籍搖滾名人堂,並獲葛萊美終身成就獎,且為時代雜誌選為「百大影響力人物」。

● 我全部的藝術生命總離不開變、變、變、前進、前進。那是唯一我感興趣的事兒。

My whole artistic life has always been about change, change, change, move on, move on. It's the only thing I find interesting.

● 如果你能將幽默與嚴肅熔於一爐,就等於已自創一格,而那也就是我夢寐以求的境界,因為你若裝模作樣,就一無是處了。

If you can get humor and seriousness at the same time, you've created a special little thing, and that's what I'm looking for, because if you get pompous, you lose everything.

● 人們經常稱我們為完美主義者,然而我們卻不是在追求完美,我們是在追求音樂中的某種魔法。

People often called us perfectionists, but we were not looking for perfection. We were looking for some kind of magic in the music.

● 火車的汽笛聲中有一種非常浪漫、懷鄉以及充滿希望的東西。

There's something about the sound of a train that's very romantic and nostalgic and hopeful.

- 我們能活下去，是靠著我們相信自己的人生會變得更好。

  We've survived by believing our life is going to get better.

- 我做這一行不是為了錢，我愛音樂，我愛作曲，我無法想像自己不去彈奏、演唱或作曲。要是不過這樣的生活，我就一定會發瘋。

  I'm not in it for the money. I like music. I love to write music. I can't imagine myself not playing or singing or writing. It would just drive me crazy if I didn't.

- 有些人從不說「我愛你」幾個字，但就如兒童一樣，他們渴望人家如此表示。

  Some people never say those words: "I love you" But, like a child, they're longing to be told.

- 要傾聽寂靜之聲。

  Listen to the sound of silence.

- 人們只去看自己想看的，其餘皆視而不見。

  A man sees what he wants to see, and disregards the rest.

# 罕醉克斯 （Jimi Hendrix, 1942-1970）

美國吉他手、歌手和作曲家，崛起於60年代初期，跟當時許多著名靈歌歌手和樂隊合作過，聲名如日中天，被公認為整個西方搖滾樂歷史上最偉大的電吉他手。他將搖滾吉他和爵士鼓融入黑人福音音樂和藍調音樂中，再以其毫不修飾的嗓音唱出充滿感情的歌曲。一生只錄製過三部專輯。

● 藍調易彈，卻難感覺。

Blues is easy to play, but hard to feel.

● 生命的故事比一眨眼還快，愛情故事不過是「哈囉」、「再見」。

The story of life is quicker then the blink of an eye, the story of love is hello, goodbye.

● 你必須給人們一些可以夢想的東西。

You have to give people something to dream on.

● 輪到我死的時候，就非死不可，所以讓我過我自己想過的人生吧。

I'm the one that has to die when it's time for me to die, so let me live my life, the way I want to.

● 有人模仿我模仿得入木三分，我聽說人們連我的錯誤都去模仿。

I've been imitated so well I've heard people copy my mistakes.

- 若說我是自由的，那是因為我一直在奔馳。

  If I'm free, it's because I'm always running.


- 音樂不會說謊，若說世上有什麼會改變，也只有經由音樂一途才能發生。

  Music doesn't lie. If there is something to be changed in this world, then it can only happen through music.


- 音樂是我的宗教。

  Music is my religion.


- 我的目標就是做一個音樂人，只把我全部的生命奉獻給這種藝術。

  My goal is to be one with the music. I just dedicate my whole life to this art.


- 與他人在一起，你必須留短髮、打領帶，所以我們正努力開創一個第三世界，你懂得我的意思吧？

  To be with the others, you have to have your hair short and wear ties. So we're trying to make a third world happen, you know what I mean?


- 我死的時候，我希望人們彈奏我的音樂，放浪形骸的狂歡，盡情宣洩。

  When I die, I want people to play my music, go wild and freak out and do anything they want to do.

# 瑪丹娜 (Madonna, 1958- )

美國流行歌手、唱片和電影製作者、舞者、演員及時裝的象徵，有「百變女王」之稱。25歲時即推出首張與名字同名的專輯，目前不僅是世界上唱片銷量最高的女藝人，也是舉世最會賺錢的樂壇天后，曾經接連有25首歌曲榮登十大最佳單曲排行榜榜首，迄今已獲得三次葛萊美獎，亦是MTV歷史上得獎最多的藝人。

● 我喜歡設想自己是帶人們去旅遊，不僅是提供娛樂，而且是在散場時帶給他們一些東西去回味。

I'd like to think I am taking people on a journey; I am not just entertaining people, but giving them something to think about when they leave.

● 許多人不敢說出自己的願望，那也就是為何他們無法如願以償的原因。

A lot of people are afraid to say what they want. That's why they don't get what they want.

● 寧可當一年老虎，也不要當百年綿羊。

Better to live one year as a tiger, than a hundred as a sheep.

● 我就是我自己的實驗，我就是我自己的藝術品。

I am my own experiment. I am my own work of art.

● 我認為每個人一生至少要結一次婚，這樣你才會瞭解那是多麼愚蠢、過時的制度。

I think that everyone should get married at least once, so you can see what a silly, outdated institution it is.

- 我代表著表達的自由，亦即落實自己的信念，追尋自己的夢想。

  I stand for freedom of expression, doing what you believe in, and going after your dreams.

- 不能因為我在大庭廣眾前寬衣解帶，就解讀成我已展露自己吋吋靈魂。

  Because I've taken my clothes off in public doesn't mean that I've revealed every inch of my soul.

- 被愛使你青春永駐。

  Being loved keeps you young.

- 我願學做甘地、金恩、藍儂，但我還要命。

  I want to be like Gandhi and Martin Luther King and John Lennon- but I want to stay alive.

- 要名氣大到得像上帝一樣，我才會快樂。

  I won't be happy till I'm as famous as God.

# 麥可傑克森 (Michael Jackson, 1958-2009)

美國搖滾樂國際巨星、作曲家、舞蹈家、唱片製作人。與貓王普里斯萊、披頭四並列為流行樂史上最偉大的象徵，享有「流行音樂之王」的美譽。1982年發行的專輯「顫慄」，全球銷售破1億張，榮登「金氏世界紀錄」上最賣座的唱片專輯，美國國會圖書館特將該專輯選為「國家寶藏」。一生獲得無數殊榮，包括13座葛萊美獎、兩度入選搖滾名人堂等。

- 在充滿遺憾的世界，我們仍須勇於期待；在充滿憤怒的世界，我們仍須勇於撫慰；在充滿絕望的世界，我們仍須勇於夢想；在充滿猜忌的世界，我們仍須勇於信任。

  In a world filled with hate, we must still dare to hope. In a world filled with anger, we must still dare to comfort. In a world filled with despair, we must still dare to dream. And in a world filled with distrust, we must still dare to believe.

- 如果你來到這個世界時，知道被人所愛，去世時亦有同感，那麼，發生在生死之間的一切事情，也就無所謂了。

  If you enter this world knowing you are loved and you leave this world knowing the same, then everything that happens in between can be dealt with.

- 我們父母教我們一定要敬業，不管做任何事都應全力以赴，要做冠軍，而非亞軍。

  Our parents taught us to always be respectful and, no matter what you do, to give it everything you have. Be the best, not the second best.

- 不能只因為它被印出來，就意味著它是真理。

  Just because it's in print doesn't mean it's the gospel.

- 你永遠可以夢想，你的夢想將成真，但你必須促使它們成真。

  You can always dream, and your dreams will come true, but you have to make them come true.

- 我對什麼事都不滿意，我是完美主義者，那是我本性的一部分。

  I'm never pleased with anything, I'm a perfectionist, it's part of who I am.

- 人們寫負面的東西，因為他們覺得那有賣點，對他們而言，好消息賣不出去。

  People write negatives things, cause they feel that's what sells. Good news to them, doesn't sell.

- 當我看到小朋友，就等於看到上帝的臉，那就是為何我那麼愛他們的原因，而那也就是我所看到的。

  When I see children, I see the face of God. That's why I love them so much. That's what I see.

- 謊言跑短程，真相跑馬拉松，真相會在法院裡贏得這場馬拉松。

  Lies run sprints, but the truth runs marathons. The truth will win this marathon in court.

- 在我內心，我將永遠是那小飛俠彼得潘。

  I'll always be Peter Pan in my heart.

# 政治界

# 湯馬斯摩爾 (Thomas More, 1478-1535)

英國著名政治家、文藝復興時期英國最偉大的人文主義思想家。其著作《烏托邦》描繪一個理想未來社會的情況，因此被認為是空想社會主義的先驅。身為英王亨利八世之重臣，因強烈反對國王擅兼國教之主，被判叛國，而走上斷頭台。名片《良相佐國》，即是刻畫其堅守風骨的感人故事。

● 所謂絕對嶄新的觀念，世所未聞。

An absolutely new idea is one of the rarest things known to man.

● 在這兒帶來你受傷的心，在這兒說出你的痛苦；人間沒有什麼悲傷是上天無法治療的。

Here bring your wounded hearts, here tell your anguish; Earth has no sorrow that Heaven cannot heal.

● 教育不是堆積學問、資訊、資料、事實、技術或能力等屬於訓練或傳習之事，而是讓隱若種子般的東西彰顯出來。

Education is not the piling on of learning, information, data, facts, skills, or abilities - that's training or instruction - but is rather making visible what is hidden as a seed.

● 我們這個時代最大問題之一就是，上學的人很多，但受過教育的人極少。

One of the greatest problems of our time is that many are schooled but few are educated.

● 懂得何時折返，就是最會旅行的人。

He travels best that knows when to return.

- 律師，是一種遮掩事情的行業。

  Lawyers-a profession it is to disguise matters.

- 友情如愛情，必然溫暖；愛情如友情，必然穩定。

  A friendship like love is warm; a love like friendship is steady.

- 如果你願意，你可以打破、可以砸碎這隻花瓶，但玫瑰的香氣仍將久久不去。

  You may break, you may shatter the vase, if you will, but the scent of the roses will hang round it still.

- 如果名譽讓人有利可圖，人人都會是正人君子。

  If honor were profitable, everybody would be honorable.

- 溫馨的回憶，給他日的我帶來光亮。

  Fond memory brings the light of other days around me.

# 派屈克亨利 (Patrick Henry, 1736-1799)

美國立國期間政治家、演說家，兩度擔任維吉尼亞州州長。1775年3月23日，亨利在李奇蒙聖約翰教堂發表《不自由，毋寧死》（Give me liberty or give me death）歷史性演說，大大鼓舞了當時英屬北美十三州人民決心脫離英國統治的士氣，有助催生美國獨立革命，因而被史家列為開國元勳。

- 憲法不是政府約束民眾的工具，它是人民約束政府的工具，以防政府主宰我們的生活與權益。

  The Constitution is not an instrument for the government to restrain the people, it is an instrument for the people to restrain the government - lest it come to dominate our lives and interests.

- 任何民族無法保有自由的政府或自由的福祉，除非堅守公義、中庸、節制、簡樸與美德，以及不斷奉行基本的原則。

  No free government, or the blessings of liberty, can be preserved to any people but by a firm adherence to justice, moderation, temperance, frugality, and virtue; and by a frequent recurrence to fundamental principles.

- 我喜歡未來的夢想，勝過喜歡過去的歷史。

  I like dreams of the future better than the history of the past.

- 聖經抵得過世上所出版的一切其他書籍。

  The Bible is worth all the other books which have ever been printed.

- 就我而言，不論精神上要承受多大的痛苦，我都寧願知道全部的真相，做最壞的打算。

  For my part, whatever anguish of spirit it may cost, I am willing to know the whole truth; to know the worst and provide for it.

- 我只有一盞引導我行路的明燈，那就是經驗之燈。

  I have but one lamp by which my feet are guided, and that is the lamp of experience.

- 除卻仰靠過去之外，我別無他法判斷未來。

  I know no way of judging the future but by the past.

- 現在我已把全部的財產留給家人，我希望我還能再給他們一樣東西，那就是基督教信仰。

  I have now disposed of all my property to my family. There is one thing more I wish I could give them, and that is the Christian religion.

- 壞人不能成為好公民。

  Bad men cannot make good citizens.

- 不自由，*毋寧死*。

  Give me liberty or give me death.

# 羅斯福 ( Theodore Roosevelt, 1858-1919 )

美國第三十二任總統，1933年至1945年期間連任四屆，被視為美國歷史上最偉大的總統之一，也是美國歷史上唯一連任4屆總統的人。執政後，以「百日新政」順利化解經濟危機。第二次世界大戰時帶領美國參戰加入同盟國，使戰局產生關鍵變化而最終打敗軸心國，1941年與英國首相邱吉爾舉行大西洋會議，共同起草《大西洋憲章》，1942年推動建立聯合國。

- 在歷史上，從來就沒有人能過安逸的一生，卻留下值得懷念的名聲。

  Never throughout history has a man who lived a life of ease left a name worth remembering.

- 若非有戰爭，就不會有偉大的將領；若非有大時機，就不會有偉大的政治家；林肯若活在承平之時，也會沒沒無聞。

  If there is not the war, you don't get the great general; if there is not a great occasion, you don't get a great statesman; if Lincoln had lived in a time of peace, no one would have known his name.

- 成功之道的最重要的單一要素，就是知道如何與他人相處。

  The most important single ingredient in the formula of success is knowing how to get along with people.

- 沒有人高過法律，也沒有人低於法律。

  No man is above the law, and no man is below it.

- 相信自己能做到，就等於已達成了一半。

  Believe you can and you're halfway there.

- 我只是一個中等之資的人，但說實在的，我比中等人來得打拼。

  I am only an average man but, by George, I work harder at it than the average man.

- 失敗固然不好受，但從未追求成功卻更不可取。

  It is hard to fail, but it is worse never to have tried to succeed.

- 人們問領袖與老闆兩者有何不同，那就是領袖懂得帶領，老闆只曉得鞭策。

  People ask the difference between a leader and a boss. The leader leads, and the boss drives.

- 老年就跟人生其他每一樁事一樣，要想過得不錯，就得從年輕開始打算。

  Old age is like everything else. To make a success of it, you've got to start young.

- 選票就像步槍，其用處仰賴使用者的品格。

  A vote is like a rifle; its usefulness depends upon the character of the user.

- 眼睛要注視著星辰，雙腳卻要站穩於地。

  Keep your eyes on the stars, and your feet on the ground.

# 麥克阿瑟 (Douglas MacArthur, 1880-1964)

美國陸軍五星上將，世人尊稱其「麥帥」。1919年出任西點軍校有史以來最年輕的校長，二次世界大戰期間率領美軍攻佔菲律賓，戰績彪炳。韓戰爆發，麥帥奉命指揮聯軍作戰，因其繼續北進之主張和杜魯門總統意見相左，因而被杜氏解職。麥帥應邀到華府國會發表演說，受到英雄式歡迎，成為其一生中最光榮之事跡。

● 你年輕於信仰，衰老於疑惑；年輕於自信，衰老於恐懼；年輕於希望，衰老於絕望。

You are as young as your faith, as old as your doubt; as young as your self-confidence, as old as your fear; as young as your hope, as old as your despair.

● 責任、榮譽、國家，這三個神聖之詞，凜然支配著你應何去何從、你能有何作為、你將如何發展。

Duty, Honor, Country. Those three hallowed words reverently dictate what you ought to be, what you can be, what you will be.

● 在戰爭中，輸贏生死之別，僅在瞬間。

In war, you win or lose, live or die - and the difference is just an eyelash.

● 年紀使形體產生皺紋，放棄卻使心靈產生皺紋。

Age wrinkles the body. Quitting wrinkles the soul.

● 老兵永遠不死，他們只是逐漸隱退。

Old soldiers never die; they just fade away.

- 人世間並無安全可言，有的只是機會而已。

  There is no security on this earth; there is only opportunity.

- 我們並非撤退，我們是從另一方向轉進。

  We are not retreating. We are advancing in another direction.

- 規則通常就是用來讓人打破，而且往往也會讓懶人藏身於後。

  Rules are mostly made to be broken and are too often for the lazy to hide behind.

- 論職業我是軍人，且以此為榮，但我更以身為人父為榮。

  By profession I am a soldier and take pride in that fact, but I am prouder to be a father.

- 永遠不要下達無法遵行的命令。

  Never give an order that can't be obeyed.

# 梅爾夫人 (Golda Meir, 1898-1978)

以色列開國元勳和第四任總理。幼年時，隨全家移居美國威斯康辛州的密爾瓦基，後來成為密城猶太復國主義工黨領導人。二次大戰期間，與英國當局進行談判，成為猶太復國運動的代言人。1948年，參加簽署以色列獨立宣言。1969年，出任以國總理，維持各黨聯合政府，呼籲通過外交手段和平解決中東問題。晚年著有自傳《我的一生》。

- 人們不能，也不應該企圖抹煞過去，只因為它與現在格格不入。

  One cannot and must not try to erase the past merely because it does not fit the present.

- 不必如此謙虛，你沒有那麼偉大。

  Don't be so humble, you're not that great.

- 我絕不是單槍匹馬的做事，在這個國家中不管有何建樹，都是糾合眾人之力。

  I never did anything alone. Whatever was accomplished in this country was accomplished collectively.

- 我可以誠實的說，我從未受一件事的成敗問題所影響。如果我覺得那是該做的事，就會不計後果的去推動。

  I can honestly say that I was never affected by the question of the success of an undertaking. If I felt it was the right thing to do, I was for it regardless of the possible outcome.

- 悲觀，是猶太人絕不可讓自己擁有的奢侈品。

  Pessimism is a luxury that a Jew can never allow himself.

- 我不能說女人是否比男人優秀，但我敢說，她們一定不比男人差。

  Whether women are better than men I cannot say - but I can say they are certainly no worse.

- 你無法與緊握著的拳頭握手。

  You cannot shake hands with a clenched fist.

- 老年就像一架穿越暴風雨的飛機，你一旦登機，也只能聽天由命了。

  Old age is like a plane flying through a storm. Once you're aboard, there's nothing you can do.

- 人長得不漂亮，是真正的福氣，因為人不漂亮迫使我開發自己內在的資源。

  Not being beautiful was the true blessing. Not being beautiful forced me to develop my inner resources.

- 那些不懂得如何盡情哭泣的人，也不會懂得如何開懷大笑。

  Those who don't know how to weep with their whole heart, don't know how to laugh either.

# 哈瑪紹（Dag Hammarskjöld, 1905-1961）

瑞典外交家和作家，從1953年4月到逝世前擔任聯合國秘書長。父親亞爾馬・哈瑪紹於1914年到1917年間擔任瑞典首相，其家族從十七世紀開始就為瑞典王室服務。1954年獲選為瑞典學院成員，1961年仍在世時獲提名諾貝爾和平獎，並於同年去世後追授。1963年他的日記式作品《路標》（Vägmärken）出版，書中記錄了1925年起至去世前的每天自省。

● 那些訴諸歷史的人，也一定會被歷史聽見，他們必須接受歷史的公斷。

Those who invoke history will certainly be heard by history. And they will have to accept its verdict.

● 所謂命運，是既無法隨心所欲，也無法迴避的東西，它是一種與常理並不相違的神祕，因為，它意味著，這個世界跟人類歷史的軌跡都是有意義的。

Destiny is something not to be desired and not to be avoided. a mystery not contrary to reason, for it implies that the world, and the course of human history, have meaning.

● 不要尋找死亡，死亡會找上你，然而，要去尋找使死亡成為一種成就的道路。

Do not seek death. Death will find you. But seek the road which makes death a fulfillment.

● 「免於恐懼的自由」一語，可以用來總結全部的人權哲學。

"Freedom from fear" could be said to sum up the whole philosophy of human rights.

- 但願我可以成長得更堅定、更單純、更內斂、更溫暖。

  If only I may grow: firmer, simpler, quieter, warmer.

- 在沒有攀上山頂之前,絕不要衡量一座山的高度,登頂之後你才會知道它有多低。

  Never measure the height of a mountain until you have reached the top. Then you will see how low it was.

- 做得愈多,就愈能做事;愈忙碌,就愈有空閒。

  The more we do, the more we can do; the more busy we are, the more leisure we have.

- 你愈忠誠的傾聽內心的聲音,就愈聽得清楚外在的發聲。

  The more faithfully you listen to the voices within you, the better you will hear what is sounding outside.

- 我們無從選擇本身命運的框架,但要把什麼東西擺進去,卻得看我們自己。

  We are not permitted to choose the frame of our destiny. But what we put into it is ours.

- 忘記任何經驗是最划不來的事,就算那是最痛苦的經驗也一樣。

  We cannot afford to forget any experience, not even the most painful.

# 歐巴馬 (Barack Obama, 1961- )

美國第44任總統。他的當選造就了美國史上第一位黑人總統。1988年，進入哈佛大學法學院深造，成為院刊《哈佛法學評論》首位非裔主編。1996年當選伊利諾州參議員，2004年當選國會參議員，成為美國國會史上第5位黑人參議員。他在競選中以「變革」為主題，主張結束伊拉克戰爭、實現能源自給等，普獲選民支援。

● 要是我們等待其他人或其他時候，改變就不會出現。我們就是自己在等待的人，我們就是自己在尋求的改變。

Change will not come if we wait for some other person or some other time. We are the ones we've been waiting for. We are the change that we seek.

● 如果你走上正確的路，而且願意繼續走下去，終究會有所進展。

If you're walking down the right path and you're willing to keep walking, eventually you'll make progress.

● 唯有胸懷超越自我的大志，你才能瞭解自己真正的潛力。

It's only when you hitch your wagon to something larger than yourself that you will realize your true potential.

● 這兒不存在自由派美國與保守派美國，只有美利堅合眾國；也不存在黑人美國、白人美國、拉丁族裔美國與亞洲人美國，只有美利堅合眾國。

There is not a liberal America and a conservative America; there is the United States of America. There is not a black America and a white America and Latino America and Asian America; there's the United States of America.

- 若是我們不願意為自己的價值觀付出代價，我們就應該捫心自問是否真對其深信不疑。

  If we aren't willing to pay a price for our values, then we should ask ourselves whether we truly believe in them at all.

- 人們並未期待政府解決一切問題，但他們深切體認到，只要在施政的優先順序上稍做調整，就能確保美國的每個小孩都有像樣的人生目標，而且機會之門就會向所有的人敞開，他們知道我們能表現得更好。

  People don't expect government to solve all their problems. But they sense, deep in their bones, that with just a slight change in priorities, we can make sure that every child in America has a decent shot at life, and that the doors of opportunity remain open to all. They know we can do better.

- 我希望這個國家能少一點律師，多一點工程師。

  I wish this country had fewer lawyers and more engineers.

- 金錢不是唯一的解答，但它使事情改觀。

  Money is not the only answer, but it makes a difference.

- 首先我要做的，就是對投票給我的人說聲謝謝，那些沒投票給我的人，我會在下一次得到你的票。

  My first job is to say thank you to those who voted me. Those who didn't, I'm going to get your vote next time.

# 文學界

# 赫伯特 (George Herbert, 1593-1633)

英國宗教詩歌作家,被歸類為玄學派詩人。他的作品描寫生動,使用隱喻出神入化。詩作大多是在晚年寫成,去世前出版的詩集《聖殿》,計收短詩160首,散文作品有《寺廟的牧師》。赫氏一生堅持用一種精準的語言從事創作,因而詩作語言直樸,意象清新,往往能在平易中蘊含著深意,此種深入淺出的詩風,乃成為其不凡的藝術特色。

- 不要等待,因為世上永遠不會有「正是時候」之時。就從你立足之處出發吧,使用你所可以運用的任何工具,一路上你就會找到更順手的工具。

  Do not wait; the time will never be "just right." Start where you stand, and work with whatever tools you may have at your command, and better tools will be found as you go along.

- 不能寬恕別人的人,破壞了他自己抵達天堂時必須通過的橋樑,因為每個人都需要被人寬恕。

  He that cannot forgive others, breaks the bridge over which he himself must pass if he would ever reach heaven; for everyone has need to be forgiven.

- 一個人二十歲時不漂亮,三十歲時不健壯,四十歲時不富有,五十歲時不聰明,那麼他就永遠不會漂亮、健壯、富有或聰明。

  He that is not handsome at 20, nor strong at 30, nor rich at 40, nor wise at 50, will never be handsome, strong, rich or wise.

- 世上若無小人,也就沒有偉人了。

  There would be no great men if there were no little ones.

- 跟人談話時，幽默重於機鋒，隨和重於多聞。

  In conversation, humor is worth more than wit and easiness more than knowledge.

- 好好活著，就是最好的報復。

  Living well is the best revenge.

- 沒有人知道另一個人擔子的重量。

  None knows the weight of another's burden.

- 有時，最好的收益，就是失去。

  Sometimes the best gain is to lose.

- 買家需要百隻眼睛，賣家沒長眼睛都行。

  The buyer needs a hundred eyes, the seller not one.

- 最簡短的答案，就是付諸行動。

  The shortest answer is doing.

- 愛情與咳嗽均無從掩飾。

  Love and a cough cannot be hid.

# 卡爾德隆 ( Pedro Calderon de la Barca, 1600-1681 )

西班牙17世紀劇作家、詩人。13歲開始寫劇本，20歲即被認為是傑出詩人。一生著有200多部作品，成為西班牙最著名的劇作家。作品每以強烈的宗教情懷為訴求，宣揚寄託來生的宗教觀，被譽為神學劇場泰斗。他的去世，象徵著西班牙戲劇黃金時代的結束。劇作有《人生如夢》、《薩拉梅亞鎮長》、《隱居的夫人》、《忠貞不渝的王子》等。

● 何謂人生？一場瘋狂；何謂人生？一個幻覺，一個影子，一個故事。世間最美好之事物，永嫌不足，儘管人生如夢，而夢本身只是夢而已。

What is life? A madness. What is life? An illusion, a shadow, a story. And the greatest good is little enough; for all life is a dream, and dreams themselves are only dreams.

● 絕不要在紙上洩露你的祕密，那就像向空中丟一塊石頭，就算你知道是誰丟的，也不曉得它會落於何方。

Never confide your secrets to paper; it is like throwing a stone in the air; and if you know who throws the stone, you do not know where it may fall.

● 未經考驗過的美德不真，只有在爐缸中的黃金才純；磁石試驗鋼鐵，鑽石測驗鑽石，金屬在爐火中才更閃亮。

No virtue can be real that has not been tried. The gold in the crucible alone is perfect; the loadstone tests the steel, and the diamond is tried by the diamond, while metals gleam the brighter in the furnace.

● 夢，是醒時靈魂的草樣。

Dreams are rough copies of the waking soul.

- 紅顏一向薄命，因為幸福與美麗格格不入。

  The dower of great beauty has always been misfortune, since happiness and beauty do not agree together.


- 愛情若不瘋狂，它就不是愛情。

  When love is not madness, it is not love.


- 人們也許懂得如何贏取勝利，卻不懂得如何善用勝利。

  One may know how to gain a victory, and know not how to use it.


- 就算在夢中，善行也不唐捐。

  For even in dreams a good deed is not lost.


- 一切都必須向歲月臣服，對時間而言，攻無不克。

  All must yield to the weight of years; conquest is not difficult for time.

# 史威夫特 (Jonathan Swift, 1667-1745)

愛爾蘭出生的英國文學家，是西方世界最傑出的散文作家。成名之作為《格列佛遊記》，是其眾多作品中最膾炙人口者。書中借托船長格列佛之口，描述四次航海中的奇異經歷，對英國當時之政治制度與現實社會極盡諷刺之能事。此外，他還寫有《桶的故事》，《書的戰爭》、《一個澡盆的故事》、《一個小小的建議》等。

● 我們有足夠的信仰讓我們懷恨，卻沒有足夠的信仰讓我們相愛。

We have enough religion to make us hate, but not enough to make us love one another.

● 權力本身不是好事，除非是用在保護好人身上。

Power is no blessing in itself, except when it is used to protect the innocent.

● 禮貌之為用，就是使跟我們交談的人，有賓至如歸之感，凡使最少人感到不安者，就是屋內最有教養的人。

Good manners is the art of making those people easy with whom we converse. Whoever makes the fewest people uneasy is the best bred in the room.

● 沒有比諂媚更失禮的事，你若諂媚所有的人，你誰也討好不到；你若諂媚一兩位，你會得罪其他人。

Nothing is so great an example of bad manners as flattery. If you flatter all the company, you please none; If you flatter only one or two, you offend the rest.

- 在適當地點使用適當話語，就是「格調」的精義。

  The proper words in the proper places are the true definition of style.

- 所謂遠見，就是那種看到別人所看不到的本領。

  Vision is the art of seeing what is invisible to others.

- 政治，一如眾所周知的，就是腐化而已。

  Politics, as the word is commonly understood, are nothing but corruptions.

- 法律有如蛛網，可以捕獲小蒼蠅，卻讓大小黃蜂穿網而過。

  Laws are like cobwebs, which may catch small flies, but let wasps and hornets break through.

- 一個敵人的為害，要大過十個朋友的嘉惠。

  One enemy can do more hurt than ten friends can do good.

# 海涅 (Heinrich Heine, 1797-1856)

德國十九世紀最偉大的抒情詩人、思想家和評論家。每以平易近人的詞句,創作出思想深刻、生動優美的詩篇,德國浪漫主義詩歌在他筆下發揮到極致。擅將報刊上的文藝專欄和遊記提升為藝術形式,賦予德語優美動人的風格。其政治詩和諷刺詩,頗能揭示其捍衛民主自由思想的理念。作品有《德國,一個冬天的童話》、《詩歌集》、《北海集》、《旅行速寫》等。

● 一場革命不論成敗,總有胸懷遠大的人為其犧牲。

Whether a revolution succeeds or fails people of great hearts will always be sacrificed to it.

● 對於自身的缺點,我們會不斷自我欺騙,直到最後我們把它們當成美德看待。

We keep on deceiving ourselves in regard to our faults, until we at last come to look upon them as virtues.

● 婚禮進行曲,總讓我想起軍人上戰場時所奏的音樂。

The Wedding March always reminds me of the music played when soldiers go into battle.

● 每個人或基於恐懼,或基於心安,都有一定的宗教情懷。

Every man, either to his terror or consolation, has some sense of religion.

● 上帝理當寬恕我,那可是祂的職責。

Of course God will forgive me; that's His job.

- 英雄一下臺，小丑就當道。

  When the heroes go off the stage, the clowns come on.

- 世間根本之惡，就源於上帝未能創造足夠的金錢。

  The fundamental evil of the world arose from the fact that the good Lord has not created money enough.

- 「經驗」是好學校，但學費高昂。

  Experience is a good school. But the fees are high.

- 睡眠是好事，死亡更不賴，但無疑的，最好是根本從未出生。

  Sleep is good, death is better; but of course, the best thing would to have never been born at all.

- 女人既是蘋果，也是毒蛇。

  Woman is at once apple and serpent.

- 不要問我擁有什麼，而要問我是怎麼樣的人。

  Ask me not what I have, but what I am.

# 屠格涅夫 (Ivan Turgenev, 1818-1883)

俄國十九世紀現實主義小說家、詩人和劇作家，與托爾斯泰、杜斯妥也夫斯基並列為俄國三大小說家。他在文學上獲有極高成就，舉凡詩歌、小說、戲劇無所不能。為文喜用第一人稱來講述故事及描寫人物心理，長篇小說《羅亭》、《貴族之家》、《父與子》、《前夜》、《煙》、《處女地》，奠定其文壇不朽的地位。所寫《獵人筆記》，為俄羅斯苦難農民代言，亦是其傳世之作。

● 時間有時像小鳥般飛馳，有時像蝸牛般爬行，但一個人若根本不會注意到時間消逝的快慢，他就是最幸福的人了。

Time sometimes flies like a bird, sometimes crawls like a snail; but a man is happiest when he does not even notice whether it passes swiftly or slowly.

● 造化無視於人類的邏輯，它自有其理則，我們卻不認得、不承認它，直到喪命於其輪下。

Nature cares nothing for logic, our human logic: she has her own, which we do not recognize and do not acknowledge until we are crushed under its wheel.

● 你可能會與某些人長久生活在一起，關係友善，卻從未真心與其交談。

You may live a long while with some people and be on friendly terms with them and never speak openly with them from your soul.

● 不論一個人在祈禱什麼，他都在祈求奇蹟的出現。

Whatever a man prays for, he prays for a miracle.

- 自身一無所求、一無所盼，對他人卻深懷同情，這才是真正的崇高。

  To desire and expect nothing for oneself and to have profound sympathy for others is genuine holiness.

- 死亡是一則老笑話，但每一個人都是初次與其邂逅。

  Death's an old joke, but each individual encounters it anew.

- 我們受限於環境，被其逼上某路，卻因而受罰。

  Circumstances define us; they force us onto one road or another, and then they punish us for it.

- 「明天」一詞，是為優柔寡斷者與兒童所發明。

  The word tomorrow was invented for indecisive people and for children.

- 忠於自己，人生全部精義就在於此。

  Belonging to oneself--the whole essence of life lies in that.

- 不管你如何扣問上天，它從不會用你可理解的語言回應。

  However much you knock at nature's door, she will never answer you in comprehensible words.

# T. S. 艾略特 (T. S. Eliot, 1888-1965)

美裔英國詩人、評論家、劇作家，1948年諾貝爾文學獎得主，作品對當代英美文學影響深遠，在文化批評方面亦多貢獻。創作有《荒原》、《四個四重奏》、《岩石》、《大教堂中的謀殺》、《當代文學的傳統和嘗試》等。其中長詩《荒原》最是膾炙人口，被稱為現代詩的里程碑。

● 一齣戲劇應給你一些東西思索，看一齣戲，第一次就能看懂的話，我就知道它無足可觀。

A play should give you something to think about. When I see a play and understand it the first time, then I know it can't be much good.

● 真正的詩，能在被瞭解之前就發揮溝通的力量。

Genuine poetry can communicate before it is understood.

● 不成熟的詩人模仿，成熟的詩人剽竊。

Immature poets imitate; mature poets steal.

● 詩人最重要的事，就是盡可能少寫。

The most important thing for poets to do is to write as little as possible.

● 只有那些甘冒走過頭之險者，才有可能發現究竟自己能走多遠。

Only those who will risk going too far can possibly find out how far one can go.

- 唯有在實物的世界裡，我們才擁有時間、空間與我們自己。

  It is only in the world of objects that we have time and space and selves.

- 讓我們不要做一個心胸狹窄、難纏、負面的人。

  Let's not be narrow, nasty, and negative.

- 諾貝爾獎是一個人自己葬禮的入場券，沒有人在得獎後仍有所作為。

  The Nobel is a ticket to one's own funeral. No one has ever done anything after he got it.

- 人類負荷不起多少現實。

  Humankind cannot bear very much reality.

- 有些編輯是失敗的作家，但大部分的作家亦復如此。

  Some editors are failed writers, but so are most writers.

- 電視是娛樂的媒介，讓千萬人同時聽見同一笑話，卻也讓他們依然孤寂。

  Television is a medium of entertainment which permits millions of people to listen to the same joke at the same time, and yet remain lonesome.

# 福婁拜 (Gustave Flaubert, 1821-1880)

法國19世紀寫實主義文學大師。中學時代開始寫作，深受悲觀主義世界觀的影響，1843至1845年間完成首部長篇小說《情感教育》，惟為求完美，一再修潤，直到1869年才定稿出版。福婁拜的寫作態度極為嚴謹，花四年多才完成的《包法利夫人》，是其另一代表作。傳世作品尚有《聖安東尼的誘惑》、《薩朗寶》、《三故事》等。

- 作家在其書中，要像上帝在宇宙中一樣，無所不在，卻又無處可見。

  The author in his book must be like God in his universe, everywhere present and nowhere visible.

- 寫作是過像狗一樣的生活，但也是唯一值得過的生活。

  Writing is a dog's life, but the only life worth living.

- 你可以從敵人的多寡，計算一個人的價值，也可以從人們撻伐一件藝術作品的情形，計算它的重要性。

  You can calculate the worth of a man by the number of his enemies, and the importance of a work of art by the harm that is spoken of it.

- 人們可以做其行為的主人，卻絕無法做其感覺的主人。

  One can be the master of what one does, but never of what one feels.

- 人們不應向蘋果樹要橘子，向法國要陽光，向女人要愛情，向人生要快樂。

  One mustn't ask apple trees for oranges, France for sun, women for love, life for happiness.

- 愚昧、自私與擁有健康的身體，是快樂的三要件，惟若缺少了愚昧，其他要件就一無用處了。

  To be stupid and selfish and to have good health are the three requirements for happiness, though if stupidity is lacking, the others are useless.

- 成功是一種結果，不應是一種目標。

  Success is a consequence and must not be a goal.

- 大地有其範圍，但人類的愚昧卻無止境。

  Earth has its boundaries, but human stupidity is limitless.

- 世上沒有真理，只有「認知」而已。

  There is no truth. There is only perception.

- 一個朋友的過世，就等於你自己身上的某一部分也隨他而去。

  A friend who dies, it's something of you who dies.

- 不要像兒童一樣，為了自娛而閱讀，或像有雄心的人那樣，為學習而閱讀。不要這樣，要為生存而閱讀。

  Do not read, as children do, to amuse yourself, or like the ambitious, for the purpose of instruction. No, read in order to live.

# 柏洛茲 ( John Burroughs, 1837-1921 )

美國散文家和自然主義者，一生都在效法梭羅的方式生活與寫作。早年做過教師、記者和農民，1871年出版第一本有關花鳥和農村景色的書《延齡草》之後，就定居哈德遜河谷，專心從事創作，後期作品顯得格外富有哲理。作品有《詩人與鳥》、《蝗蟲與野蜜》、《標誌與季節》、《自然之路》、《惠特曼研究》、《時間與變化》等。

● 一個人可以失敗很多次，然而一直到他開始責怪別人之前，他都不算是一名失敗者。

A man can fail many times, but he isn't a failure until he begins to blame somebody else.

● 對任何值得擁有的東西，人們都須付出代價，而此一代價總不外乎工作、忍耐、愛、自我犧牲。

For anything worth having one must pay the price; and the price is always work, patience, love, self-sacrifice.

● 天國，不是一個地方，而是一種心境。

The Kingdom of Heaven is not a place, but a state of mind.

● 快樂的祕訣，就是做有意義的事，也就是找尋人生的目的。

The secret of happiness is having something meaningful to do, seeking purpose.

● 人生是一場奮鬥，而不是一場戰爭。

Life is a struggle, but not a warfare.

- 樹葉老去時是何等美麗，它們最後日子的亮度跟色彩是何等飽滿。

  How beautiful the leaves grow old. How full of light and color are their last days.

- 心中必須先有鳥，你才能在林中發現其蹤影。

  You must have the bird in your heart before you can find it in the bush.

- 要學到一些新東西，就走昨天走過的小徑好了。

  To learn something new, take the path that you took yesterday.

- 對我來說，所謂老年永遠就是比現在的我再大十歲。

  To me - old age is always ten years older than I am.

- 最微不足道的行動，也要勝過最大的善念。

  The smallest deed is better than the greatest intention

# 康拉德 (Joseph Conrad, 1857-1924)

波蘭裔英國小說家，是少數以非母語寫作而能成名之作家，被譽為現代主義的先驅。年輕時當過海員、船長，對海洋生活有深刻體驗，中年才改行從事文學創作。所寫《黑暗之心》、《吉姆爺》、《救援》、《諾斯特羅莫》入選二十世紀百大英文小說。其中描寫在剛果河上航行的《黑暗之心》，是最負盛名的代表作。

● 就算是人們最公開的行動，也會有其不為人知的一面。

A man's most open actions have a secret side to them.

● 衡量一個人，要看其仇敵，也要看其朋友。

You shall judge a man by his foes as well as by his friends.

● 我有雄心，不僅比前人走得更遠，而且要遠行到人所可能到達的地方。

I had ambition not only to go farther than any man had ever been before, but as far as it was possible for a man to go.

● 談論一個人背叛其國家、朋友、情人，先須有一種道德關聯，一個人所能背叛的，無非就是他的良知而已。

They talk of a man betraying his country, his friends, his sweetheart. There must be a moral bond first. All a man can betray is his conscience.

● 當女人極不容易，因其首要之務就是跟男人打交道。

Being a woman is a terribly difficult task, since it consists principally in dealing with men.

- 沒人承認自己喜歡說人是非，然而人人都樂此不疲。

  Gossip is what no one claims to like, but everybody enjoys.


- 我們活著，一如我們作夢，都是孑然一身。

  We live, as we dream--alone.


- 不相信運氣，是涉世未深者的特徵。

  It is the mark of an inexperienced man not to believe in luck.


- 工作比玩樂更好玩。

  Work is much more fun than fun.


- 不必去相信世間存有一種超自然的邪惡源頭，單單人類就很有能力做盡惡事了。

  The belief in a supernatural source of evil is not necessary; men alone are quite capable of every wickedness.

# 巴利 （James M. Barrie, 1860-1937）

英國劇作家和小說家，創造小飛俠彼得潘力戰海盜虎克船長的故事，家喻戶曉。巴利屬於多產作家，作品有《古老輕鬆的田園詩》、《單身的時候》、《小白鳥》、《彼得潘》、《小牧師》、《婦人皆知》、《值十二英鎊的相貌》、《遺囑》以及《親愛的布魯特斯》等。1928年他成為作家協會的主席，1930年擔任愛丁堡大學的校長。

● 一定有人警告過你，不要讓黃金時光溜走，然而，有些時間之所以被視為黃金時光，正是因為我們讓其溜走。

You must have been warned against letting the golden hours slip by; but some of them are golden only because we let them slip by.

● 只要我們殷切期盼，夢想就一定成真。只要你願意犧牲其他一切去追求，你就可以得到人生的任何東西。

Dreams do come true, if we only wish hard enough, You can have anything in life if you will sacrifice everything else for it.

● 每個人的一生都是一本日記，用以記載著一個又一個的故事；在他把目前日記的分量，跟他發誓要做到的分量做一比較時，也就是他最謙卑的時刻。

The life of every man is a diary in which he means to write one story, and writes another; and his humblest hour is when he compares the volume as it is with what he vowed to make it.

● 上帝賜予我們記憶力，所以我們在十二月份還能有玫瑰。

God gave us memory so that we might have roses in December.

10558 台北市松山區八德路3段12巷57弄40號

# 九歌出版社有限公司 收

姓　名：

手　機：

e-mail：

教育程度：□國中(含以下) □高中職 □大學專科 □研究所(含以上)

與好友分享《九歌書訊雜誌》

推薦三名不同地址的好朋友，他們將分別免費獲贈《九歌書訊雜誌》

性別：男□ 女□　出生：＿＿＿年＿＿月＿＿日

電話：（　　　）

地　址：□□□

姓　名：　　　　　　　　　　　地址：□□□

姓　名：　　　　　　　　　　　地址：□□□

姓　名：　　　　　　　　　　　地址：□□□

# 隨時隨地擁有閱讀的美好時刻！

九歌文學網 http://www.chiuko.com.tw

## 讀者回函卡

謝謝您購買本書，我們非常重視您的意見與想法，請您費心填寫並寄回給我們！

● 購買的書名_____

● 購買本書最主要的原因(可以複選)：□書名 □內容 □封面設計 □價格便宜 □整體包裝 □作家

　□其他，告訴我們你的想法：_____

● 您如何發現這本書：□書店 □網路書店 □書訊 □廣告DM □報紙 □廣播 □電視 □親友介紹

　□其他_____

● 下一本你想買的書，主題會是：□華文創作 □翻譯小說 □生活風格 □少兒文學 □勵志學習
　□兩性成長 □醫療保健 □旅遊美食 □藝術人文

　□其他_____

● 您通常用哪一種方式購書：□郵購 □逛書店 □網路書店 □劃撥 □信用卡 □傳真

　□其他_____

- 小鳥會飛，我們卻不會飛的原因就是，牠們擁有十足的信心，因為擁有信心就等於擁有翅膀。

  The reason birds can fly and we can't is simply that they have perfect faith, for to have faith is to have wings.

- 那些把陽光帶進別人生命的人，自己也難免不沾滿陽光。

  Those who bring sunshine into the lives of others cannot keep it from themselves.

- 一個人的最佳死所，就是為別人而死的地方。

  The best place a person can die, is where they die for others.

- 我沒有年輕到可以無所不知。

  I am not young enough to know everything.

- 快樂的祕訣，不在於做我們喜歡的事，而在於喜歡我們所做的事。

  The secret of happiness is not in doing what one likes, but in liking what one does.

- 一個人的宗教，就是他所最有興趣的東西。

  One's religion is whatever one is most interested in.

# 葉慈 (William Butler Yeats, 1865-1939)

愛爾蘭詩人、劇作家、散文家，20世紀最偉大的英語詩人之一。早年的創作具有浪漫主義的華麗色彩，中年之後受詩人龐德以及愛爾蘭民族主義運動的影響，風格丕變，而更趨近於現代主義。詩集有《蘆葦叢中的風》、《在塞文森林裡》、《綠盔》、《盤旋的樓梯》等。1923年榮獲諾貝爾文學獎，獲獎理由是「以其高度藝術化且靈感洋溢之詩作，呈現整個民族的靈魂。」

● 這兒沒有什麼陌生人，只有你尚未見過的朋友。

There are no strangers here; Only friends you haven't yet met.

● 一行詩也許要花我們好幾小時，但它若看起來不像是出自靈光一閃，我們的字斟句酌就算白費了。

A line will take us hours maybe; Yet if it does not seem a moment's thought, our stitching and unstitching has been naught.

● 跟他人吵架，我們成就口才，但跟自己吵架，我們成就詩句。

We make out of the quarrel with others, rhetoric, but of the quarrel with ourselves, poetry.

● 當你老了，白髮蒼蒼，時有睡意，在爐邊打盹時，請取下此書，慢慢翻閱，夢想過往柔和的眼神，以及眼中深濃的陰影。

When you are old and gray and full of sleep, and nodding by the fire, take down this book and slowly read, and dream of the soft look your eyes had once, and of their shadows deep.

- 思考時要像智者，但交談時貴能平易。

  Think like a wise man but communicate in the language of the people.

- 人生是一場長期的準備，為的是一輩子也不會發生的事。

  Life is a long preparation for something that never happens.

- 若說苦難帶來智慧，我寧願少一點智慧。

  If suffering brings wisdom, I would wish to be less wise.

- 教育不是在灌輸，而是在點火。

  Education is not filling a bucket, but lighting a fire.

- 純真的人和漂亮的人沒有敵人，除了時間之外。

  The innocent and the beautiful have no enemy but time.

- 所有空虛的靈魂，都趨向於極端的意見。

  All empty souls tend toward extreme opinions.

# 梵樂希 ( Paul Valéry, 1871-1945 )

法國20世紀上半葉最偉大的詩人、傑出的批評家、法國後期象徵派大師，亦是法蘭西學院院士。除了文學作品外，他還撰寫了大量有關藝術、歷史、政治、音樂等方面的論著。其詩學思想繼承了象徵主義傳統，深富哲理，並追求形式之完美。《水仙辭》、《海濱墓園》、《年輕的命運女神》等，均是其代表作。

● 上帝造人，發現他不夠孤獨，就給其伴侶，讓他更強烈的感受到孤獨。

God created man and, finding him not sufficiently alone, gave him a companion to make him feel his solitude more keenly.

● 書籍跟人有同樣的敵人：火、溼氣、動物、天氣，以及它們本身的內容。

Books have the same enemies as people: fire, humidity, animals, weather, and their own content.

● 藝術家從未完成其作品，他只是將其棄之不顧而已。

An artist never really finishes his work, he merely abandons it.

● 在詩的世界，一切非說不可的，幾乎都不可能說得到位。

In poetry everything which must be said is almost impossible to say well.

● 商人，是舞蹈家與計算師的混血。

A businessman is a hybrid of a dancer and a calculator.

- 心理學的目的就是，讓我們對最懂的事，有一全然不同的看法。

  The purpose of psychology is to give us a completely different idea of the things we know best.

- 畫家不該是畫他所看到的，而是畫那應該被看出的。

  A painter should not paint what he sees but what should be seen.

- 偉人，就是在他去世之後，讓他人迷失的人。

  A great man is one who leaves others at a loss after he is gone.

- 所謂禮貌，就是組織過的冷漠。

  Politeness is organized indifference.

- 權力若不濫用，就失去其魅力。

  Power without abuse loses its charm.

- 所謂愛情，就是一起做笨蛋。

  Love is being stupid together.

# 史坦 ( Gertrude Stein, 1874-1946 )

美國前衛派女作家。年輕時曾追隨哲學家詹姆斯（William James）研習心理學。後來長期定居巴黎，所主持之沙龍成為藝文界人士歡聚之所。生平發表的第一本小說是《三個女人的一生》，另有長篇小說《美國人的成長》、歌劇《我們大家的母親》與《三幕劇中四聖人》等，都是其代表作。

● 歷史需要時間，歷史製造記憶。

History takes time. History makes memory.

● 臨終前，她問，答案是什麼？沒得到回應。她笑了笑，就說，既然如此，問題是什麼？說完她就死了。

Just before she died she asked, What is the answer? No answer came. She laughed and said, In that case, what is the question? Then she died.

● 獨處時，想跟別人在一起，跟別人在一起時，又想獨處。人不就是那樣。

When they are alone they want to be with others, and when they are with others they want to be alone. After all, human beings are like that.

● 作家應用眼睛寫作，畫家應用耳朵作畫。

A writer should write with his eyes and a painter paint with his ears.

● 美國是我的祖國，巴黎是我的家鄉。

America is my country and Paris is my hometown.

- 爭辯對我，就像呼吸的空氣，無論人家有啥主張，我都會情不自禁的相信其反面，而挺身辯護。

  Argument is to me the air I breathe. Given any proposition, I cannot help believing the other side and defending it.

- 我一直注意到，真正偉大的作家在畫像中，嘴巴總是緊閉的。

  I have always noticed that in portraits of really great writers the mouth is always firmly closed.

- 我曾有錢過，也曾窮過，有錢還是比較好。

  I've been rich and I've been poor. It's better to be rich.

- 每個人整天都得到如此多的資訊，以致失去其常識。

  Everybody gets so much information all day long that they lose their common sense.

- 我們的內心永遠是同一年齡。

  We are always the same age inside.

# 褚威格 (Stefan Zweig, 1881-1942)

奧地利著名小說家、傳記作家，出身於猶太家庭，擅長寫詩、隨筆、短篇小說與戲劇，對人物性格刻畫，尤為精到。先卜居薩爾斯堡，後遭納粹迫害，流亡英國，再移居巴西，因對世局極度失望，夫婦雙雙自殺。作品有《一個陌生女子的來信》、《看不見的珍藏》、《月光胡同》等。

- 然而，有創意的人，會受一種與國法迥異的較高律法約束。任何人要在工作上有所開創，任何人要有所發現或作為，藉以推進全人類的志業，其家園就不再存在於他的鄉土，而是存在於他的工作。

  But the creative person is subject to a different, higher law than mere national law. Whoever has to create a work, whoever has to bring about a discovery or deed which will further the cause of all of humanity, no longer has his home in his native land but rather in his work.

- 歷史一如人生，悔恨無法挽回逝去的片刻，千載歲月也找不回一時之間所失去的東西。

  In history as in human life, regret does not bring back a lost moment and a thousand years will not recover something lost in a single hour.

- 在歷史上，「理性」與「和解」擡頭的時刻，是短暫易逝的。

  In history, the moments during which reason and reconciliation prevail are short and fleeting.

- 每一個波浪，不管飆得多麼洶湧澎湃，終究會從其內部崩解。

  Every wave, regardless of how high and forceful it crests, must eventually collapse within itself.

- 往往一個遠離聚光燈的人，其心靈與能量的存在，決定了未來好幾世紀歷史的軌跡。

  Often the presence of mind and energy of a person remote from the spotlight decide the course of history for centuries to come.

- 唯有經歷過光明與黑暗、戰爭與和平、興起與衰亡的人，也唯有那樣的人才算真正體驗過人生。

  Only the person who has experienced light and darkness, war and peace, rise and fall, only that person has truly experienced life.

- 那種不願獻身任何教條，也不會倒向任何政黨的自由、獨立之士，在世上就沒有家園可言。

  The free, independent spirit who commits himself to no dogma and will not decide in favor of any party has no homestead on earth.

- 我們這一代的生活現已定型，我們沒有力量去影響世事的流轉，也沒有權利給下一代提出忠告。

  The life of our generation is now set. We do not have the power to influence the flow of events, and no right to offer advice to the next generation.

- 在你感受到那是一種犧牲時，去犧牲就沒有什麼道理了。

  There is no sense to a sacrifice after you come to feel that it is a sacrifice.

# 納森 (George Jean Nathan, 1882-1958)

二十世紀美國著名劇評家、專欄作家。創辦並長期主編《美國水星雜誌》、《美國觀察家雜誌》以及《黑色面具雜誌》。所寫劇評頗能言之有物，深受藝文界推崇。其著作豐富，諸如《批評家與戲劇》、《魔鏡》、《一個批評家的聖經》等，無不暢銷一時，其撰寫評論的哲學則見諸《態度的傳記》一書。

● 爛官員是不去投票的好公民所選出來的。

Bad officials are elected by good citizens who do not vote.

● 一顆破碎的心，是不朽愛情的紀念碑；如願以償，卻是垂死愛情的紀念碑。

A broken heart is a monument to a love that will never die; fulfillment is a monument to a love that is already on its deathbed.

● 男人欣賞女人，不是因為她說什麼，而是她傾聽什麼。

A man admires a woman not for what she says, but what she listens to.

● 一個樂觀主義者，就是那種相信家蠅正在找尋出路的人。

An optimist is a fellow who believes a housefly is looking for a way to get out.

● 所謂批評，即是用自己的價值觀去評價別人的一種藝術。

Criticism is the art of appraising others at one's own value.

- 我喝酒，是為讓他人看起來有意思。

  I drink to make other people interesting.

- 有人說我現在與過去講的話自相矛盾，不錯，我與時精進。

  It is also said of me that I now and then contradict myself. Yes, I improve wonderfully as time goes on.

- 沒有人在緊握拳頭時，能思慮得清楚。

  No man thinks clearly when his fists are clenched.

- 女人年紀愈大，愈仰賴化妝品；男人年紀愈大，愈仰賴幽默感。

  Women, as they grow older, rely more and more on cosmetics. Men, as they grow older, rely more and more on a sense of humor.

- 一位真正喜劇演員的考驗，就是在他張口之前，是否你已朝他笑開。

  The test of a real comedian is whether you laugh at him before he opens his mouth.

# 喬治艾略特 (George Eliot, 1819-1880)

英國維多利亞時代的小說家，她開創了現代小說經常採用的心理分析技巧。主要著作有《亞當·比德》、《河畔磨坊》、《織工馬南》、《米德爾馬奇》和《丹尼爾·狄隆達》。其中《米德爾馬奇》公認是她最重要的作品，書中眾多人物複雜交織的命運，刻畫出人類的自由意志與自由選擇，也顯示了她是一位浪漫主義的人道主義者。

● 你應該讀讀歷史，而且注意放逐、迫害、殉難那類的事情，你會明白，凡此種種總是發生在最傑出的人身上。

You should read history and look at ostracism, persecution, martyrdom, and that kind of thing. They always happen to the best men, you know.

● 生命河流中的黃金時刻，從我們身邊匆匆溜走，我們除了沙子外一無所見；天使來探視我們，我們在祂們走後才察覺。

The golden moments in the stream of life rush past us, and we see nothing but sand; the angels come to visit us, and we only know them when they are gone.

● 在隔了一段時間後，對我們而言，任何故事都不會維持不變，或更確切的說，我們這些讀故事的人，已不再是相同的詮釋者。

No story is the same to us after a lapse of time; or rather we who read it are no longer the same interpreters.

● 好個美妙的秋天！就連我的靈魂都與它難捨難分，我若是小鳥，我會到處翱翔，追尋那一個接著一個的秋天。

Delicious autumn! My very soul is wedded to it, and if I were a bird I would fly about the earth seeking the successive autumns.

- 偉大的事情不是靠衝動所完成，而是靠著把一系列小事情串聯起來。

  Great things are not done by impulse, but by a series of small things brought together.

- 我不僅希望有人愛我，也希望對方說出來。

  I like not only to be loved, but to be told I am loved.

- 天空絕不會落下玫瑰，我們要想擁有更多玫瑰，就必須栽種更多的樹。

  It will never rain roses: when we want to have more roses we must plant more trees.

- 五十歲到七十歲之間的歲月最難熬，一直有人找你做事，而你又未衰老到可以拒絕。

  The years between fifty and seventy are the hardest. You are always being asked to do things, and yet you are not decrepit enough to turn them down.

- 人生有許多勝利，要比挫敗還不如。

  There are many victories worse than a defeat.

- 面帶微笑，得到朋友；面帶愁容，得到皺紋。

  Wear a smile and have friends; wear a scowl and have wrinkles.

# 曼斯菲爾德 (Katherine Mansfield, 1888-1923)

紐西蘭裔的英國短篇小說家，現代短篇小說發展史上的核心人物，有「短篇小說大師」之稱。一生致力於短篇小說的創作與技巧革新，其人物分析首重內心世界和思想活動。作品有《在德國公寓裏》、《前奏曲》、《園會》、《航程》、《陌生人》、《她的第一個舞會》等。

- 要是我們能改變自己的態度，不僅對人生的觀照應有所不同，而且人生本身也會變得很不一樣。

  Could we change our attitude, we should not only see life differently, but life itself would come to be different.

- 孤獨是一件可怕的事，不錯，確實如此，然而千萬不要拉下你的面具，除非你在底下已備妥另一張面具，那張面具多恐怖都行，但就得是一張面具。

  It's a terrible thing to be alone - yes it is - it is - but don't lower your mask until you have another mask prepared beneath - as terrible as you like - but a mask.

- 我始終覺得友情的至高殊榮、解脫與安慰，就是我們不必做任何解釋。

  I always felt that the great high privilege, relief and comfort of friendship was that one had to explain nothing.

- 當我們可以開始嚴肅面對自己的失敗，那就意味著我們不再害怕失敗；學會自嘲，有無比重要。

  When we can begin to take our failures seriously, it means we are ceasing to be afraid of them. It is of immense importance to learn to laugh at ourselves.

- 不管何時我在準備旅行，我都好像在準備赴死一樣，萬一我再也回不來，一切都已就緒。

  Whenever I prepare for a journey I prepare as though for death. Should I never return, all is in order.

- 我先是一名作家，然後才是一個女人。

  I'm a writer first and a woman after.

- 冒險！冒任何險！不必在乎他人的意見、在乎那些聲音。去做世上最難的事，為你自己行動，要面對真理。

  Risk! Risk anything! Care no more for the opinions of others, for those voices. Do the hardest thing on earth for you. Act for yourself. Face the truth.

- 承認恐懼的存在，就等於讓失敗發生。

  To acknowledge the presence of fear is to give birth to failure.

- 人生對我來說，絕不會成為習以為常之事，它永遠都是一種驚豔。

  Life never becomes a habit to me. It's always a marvel.

- 你最想做什麼？在面對困難時，那是我必須不斷捫心自問的。

  What do you want most to do? That's what I have to keep asking myself, in the face of difficulties.

# 考克多 (Jean Cocteau, 1889-1963)

20世紀法國最重要的詩人之一，也是超現實主義藝術的先驅，同時又是集導演、劇作家、設計家、畫家、雕塑家於一身的全才藝術家。他最為人所知的作品有《美女與野獸》、《奧菲的遺言》、《阿拉丁之燈》、《引吭高歌》、《釘在十字架上》等。1955年入選為法蘭西學院院士。

● 藝術製造醜的東西，但後來經常變美；在另一方面，時尚製造美的東西，但後來總是變醜。

Art produces ugly things which frequently become more beautiful with time. Fashion, on the other hand, produces beautiful things which always become ugly with time.

● 藝術工作的報償不是名聲或成功，而是上癮，那就是何以有如此多的爛藝術家不會退場的原因。

The reward of art is not fame or success but intoxication: that is why so many bad artists are unable to give it up.

● 幾乎所有社會的本能，都是把任何真正自由的人禁閉起來。首先，社會開始想辦法打擊你，如果失敗了，就想辦法毒害你，如果也失敗了，最後只好把榮耀加諸在你頭上。

The instinct of nearly all societies is to lock up anybody who is truly free. First, society begins by trying to beat you up. If this fails, they try to poison you. If this fails too, the finish by loading honors on your head.

● 我們必須相信運氣，否則我們又如何解釋那些我們討厭的人獲得成功？

We must believe in luck. For how else can we explain the success of those we don't like?

- 對一個詩人而言，最不堪的悲劇就是，經由誤解而受到敬重。

  The worst tragedy for a poet is to be admired through being misunderstood.


- 我出生之日，我的死亡就開始啟程，它正從容不迫的朝我逼近。

  The day of my birth, my death began its walk. It is walking toward me, without hurrying.


- 在巴黎，人人都想當演員，沒人安於做一名觀眾。

  In Paris, everybody wants to be an actor; nobody is content to be a spectator.


- 風格，是表達複雜事情的簡易方法。

  Style is a simple way of saying complicated things.


- 所謂詩人，就是總是吐實的騙子。

  The poet is a liar who always speaks the truth.


- 世間有些實話是在你已贏得說的權利後，才能說出來。

  There are truths which one can only say after having won the right to say them.

# 休斯（Langston Hughes, 1902-1967）

美國文壇黑人文學的巨擘。小說、戲劇、散文、傳記各種文體，無所不能，尤以詩歌最為擅長，有「黑人民族的桂冠詩人」之美譽。創作深受其在紐約市哈林區生活的影響，成為哈林文藝復興運動中最重要的作家及思想家。作品有《歡樂》、《欲望》、《夢鄉人》、《水邊街》等。

- 要堅持夢想，如果失去夢想，人生就成了無法飛翔的折翼之鳥。

  Hold fast to dreams, for if dreams die, life is a broken winged bird that cannot fly.

- 詩人也是人，是人就須活在其時代之中，活在其國境之中，跟其同胞一起生活，也為其同胞而活。

  A poet is a human being. Each human being must live within his time, with and for his people, and within the boundaries of his country.

- 身為藝術家必須自由選擇自己所從事的，然而，他也必須永不懼怕去從事自己所選擇的。

  An artist must be free to choose what he does, certainly, but he must also never be afraid to do what he might choose.

- 所謂幽默，就是在未能稱心快意之時，笑顏以對。

  Humor is laughing at what you haven't got when you ought to have it.

- 沒有任何偉大的詩人會害怕做自己。

  No great poet has ever been afraid of being himself.

- 幽默就像可喜的夏雨，會急速滌淨及冷卻大地、空氣與你。

  Like a welcome summer rain, humor may suddenly cleanse and cool the earth, the air and you.


- 讓雨親吻你，讓雨用銀水珠敲擊你的頭，讓雨為你唱首催眠曲。

  Let the rain kiss you. Let the rain beat upon your head with silver liquid drops. Let the rain sing you a lullaby.


- 我們黑人作家，就因為是黑人，終生名列於黑名單，對我們而言，審查是從色系開始。

  We Negro writers, just by being black, have been on the blacklist all our lives. Censorship for us begins at the color line.


- 要想為你的創作開創市場，你就必須做一名堅定、專業、不斷創作的作家，而不是做一個僅僅寫一篇文章、一則故事或一本書的人。

  To create a market for your writing you have to be consistent, professional, a continuing writer - not just a one-article or a one-story or a one-book man.


- 我對人生的體悟就是，如果你真想去一個地方，總有辦法如願以償。

  I have discovered in life that there are ways of getting almost anywhere you want to go, if you really want to go.


- 我要做一個詩人，不是做一個黑人詩人。

  I want to be a poet, not a Negro poet.

# 康納利 （Cyril Connolly, 1903-1974）

英國文學評論家、小說家、文學雜誌《地平線》的創辦人和主編，以獨具個人風格的評論聞名於世。牛津大學畢業後，開始其筆耕生涯，為《觀察家》、《新政治家》、《星期日泰晤士報》等雜誌撰稿。1936年，發表其生平唯一的長篇小說《岩池》，他最著名的作品則是1938年出版的文集《希望的敵人》。

● 偉大的作家創造出一個自己的世界，讓讀者心滿意足的倘佯其間；二流作家也可以引誘讀者進來一下子，但不久就會目睹他們魚貫而出。

A great writer creates a world of his own and his readers are proud to live in it. A lesser writer may entice them in for a moment, but soon he will watch them filing out.

● 寧為自己寫作，而心無眾人，也不要為眾人寫作，而心無自己。

Better to write for yourself and have no public, than to write for the public and have no self.

● 文學作為藝術，就是寫出值得一再閱讀的東西；新聞文字瀏覽一次已足。

Literature is the art of writing something that will be read twice; journalism what will be grasped at once

● 成功的祕訣就是要與生存契合無間，永遠保持平靜，讓生命的每個浪潮把我們沖得更接近海岸一點。

The secret of success is to be in harmony with existence, to be always calm to let each wave of life wash us a little farther up the shore.

- 藝術的報酬，不是聲名或成功，而是自我陶醉：那就說明了為何這麼多爛藝術家未能放棄的原因。

  The reward of art is not fame or success but intoxication: that is why so many bad artists are unable to give it up.

- 對孤獨的懼怕，要超過對束縛的懼怕，所以我們會去結婚。

  The dread of loneliness is greater than the fear of bondage, so we get married.

- 永遠要對那些比你年輕的人客氣一點，因為他們是會寫你的人。

  Always be nice to those younger than you, because they are the ones who will be writing about you.

- 藝術家是悠閒階級的一員，但卻付不起自己的悠閒。

  The artist is a member of the leisured classes who cannot pay for his leisure.

- 所謂年輕，就是一段錯失機會的時期。

  Youth is a period of missed opportunities.

- 一個時代的文明，會變成下個時代的肥料。

  The civilization of one epoch becomes the manure of the next.

# 林白夫人 (Anne Morrow Lindbergh, 1906-2001)

美國作家、飛行家、旅行家。1933年，擔任副駕駛和無線電操作員，伴隨丈夫查爾斯·林白飛越五大洲，所寫《從北美到東方》和《聽！風聲》兩書紀錄了彼夫婦一起完成飛行的壯舉。其著作等身，本本都是她的傳世之作。

● 基本上，母親與家庭主婦都是唯一沒有固定休假的工人，她們是偉大的無休階層。

By and large, mothers and housewives are the only workers who do not have regular time off. They are the great vacationless class.

● 憂傷無法分擔，每個人都得獨自承受，以自己的方式挑起個人的負荷。

Grief can't be shared. Everyone carries it alone. His own burden in his own way.

● 無論如何我都必須把它全部寫出來，寫作就是思考，它更有甚於生活，因為它是對生活的感知。

I must write it all out, at any cost. Writing is thinking. It is more than living, for it is being conscious of living.

● 一個人不能蒐集海灘上所有美麗的貝殼，只能蒐集一些，若是稀少，它們才顯得更美。

One cannot collect all the beautiful shells on the beach. One can collect only a few, and they are more beautiful if they are few.

● 早晨插花可以在忙碌的一天中帶來一份寧靜，就像寫一首詩或做一次禱告。

Arranging a bowl of flowers in the morning can give a sense of quiet in a crowded day - like writing a poem or saying a prayer.

- 大海不會獎賞那些太急切、太貪心、太沒有耐性的人。人們應像海灘一樣，以放空、開放、無所選擇之姿，等待來自大海的禮物。

  The sea does not reward those who are too anxious, too greedy, or too impatient. One should lie empty, open, choiceless as a beach - waiting for a gift from the sea.

- 如果一個人不能觸動自己，那麼他就不能觸動別人。

  If one is out of touch with oneself, then one cannot touch others.

- 你在海邊感受到的孤獨，是私密與鮮活的，它並不會壓抑你，使你感到辛酸，而是激發孤獨。

  The loneliness you get by the sea is personal and alive. It doesn't subdue you and make you feel abject. It's stimulating loneliness.

- 得不到回報或得不到任何注意的付出，本身就具有一種與眾不同的特質。

  To give without any reward, or any notice, has a special quality of its own.

- 我覺得我們全都是汪洋大海中的孤島。

  I feel we are all islands - in a common sea.

# 帕韋澤 (Cesare Pavese, 1908-1950)

義大利著名詩人、評論家、小說家以及翻譯家。作品深受
美國19世紀作家梅爾維爾、愛爾蘭小說家喬伊斯的影響。
他是伊諾第（Einaudi）出版社的創辦人，一生都在從事於
編務與寫作，主編過反法西斯刊物《文化》。傳世之作有
《監獄》、《同志》、《苦役》、《月亮和篝火》、《美
麗的夏天》、《死神將藉你的眼睛注視著我》等。

- 在這個世界裡，人從不是完全的孤獨，最起碼，跟他作伴的還有
  一個男孩、一個少年及一個漸長的成人—也就是過去的那個他。

  A man is never completely alone in this world. At the worst,
  he has the company of a boy, a youth, and by and by a
  grown man - the one he used to be.

- 如果真有可能過一種毫無罪惡感的生活，那將是一種多麼可怕
  的真空。

  If it were possible to have a life absolutely free from every
  feeling of sin, what a terrifying vacuum it would be.

- 不處逆境，不會瞭解自己的實力。

  He knows not his own strength that hath not met adversity.

- 在面具卸下之時，人生的晚年就像一場化裝舞會的尾聲。

  The closing years of life are like the end of a masquerade
  party, when the masks are dropped.

- 人生可說苦不堪言，愛情的快慰不過是一帖麻醉劑而已。

  Life is pain and the enjoyment of love is an anesthetic.

- 生活的藝術，就是知道如何去相信謊言的藝術。

  The art of living is the art of knowing how to believe lies.

- 愛情是最廉價的宗教。

  Love is the cheapest of religions.

- 沒有人會欠缺自殺的好理由。

  No one ever lacks a good reason for suicide.

- 給我現成的手，而不是現成的舌。

  Give me the ready hand rather than the ready tongue.

- 我們記不得一天天的日子，我們記得片片段段的時光。

  We do not remember days, we remember moments.

- 每一種奢侈品都必須付出代價，而就從活在這個世界算起，無一不是奢侈品。

  Every luxury must be paid for, and everything is a luxury, starting with being in this world.

# 萊辛（Doris Lessing, 1919- ）

英國女作家、2007年諾貝爾文學獎得主。瑞典皇家學院在宣佈得獎人的頌詞中讚美她是「一位女性經驗的史詩作家，以其懷疑精神、激情和遠見，讓一個四分五裂的文明接受檢驗」，確實能一針見血的總結萊辛長期對女性權益、種族平等、政治議題的深沉關懷。作品有《金色筆記》、《青草在歌唱》、《生還者回憶錄》、《老酋長的故鄉》、《芳鄰日記》等。

- 我不太懂創意寫作課程，不過，如果他們不教導：第一，寫作是辛苦的工作；第二，要當作家，你必須放棄人生很多東西，也就是放棄你的私生活，那麼，他們就沒有跟你講實話。

  I don't know much about creative writing programs. But they're not telling the truth if they don't teach, one, that writing is hard work, and, two, that you have to give up a great deal of life, your personal life, to be a writer.

- 我認為，我們之所以看重敘事文字，是因為其型式已深入腦海，我們的大腦已習於接納故事性及連續性的東西。

  It is my belief that we value narrative because the pattern is in our brain. Our brains are patterned for storytelling, for the consecutive.

- 你只能靠實際去寫作，學習成為一名較好的作家。

  You only learn to be a better writer by actually writing.

- 所謂學習就是，你突然瞭解到某件你一輩子一直瞭解的事，然而，是以一種嶄新的方式去瞭解。

  That is what learning is. You suddenly understand something you've understood all your life, but in a new way.

- 一切政治運動都是這樣：我們是對的，其他每個人都是錯的。在我們自己這邊的人，若跟我們意見相左，就是異端，他們開始成為敵人。久而久之，就產生一種你自認高人一等的絕對信念，於是萬事都過度簡化，而且存在著一種彈性所造成的恐怖。

  All political movements are like this -- we are in the right, everyone else is in the wrong. The people on our own side who disagree with us are heretics, and they start becoming enemies. With it comes an absolute conviction of your own moral superiority. There's oversimplification in everything, and a terror of flexibility.

- 不管任何地方的任何人，只要給予機會去表現，就能展露千百種意想不到的才華與能力。

  Any human anywhere will blossom in a hundred unexpected talents and capacities simply by being given the opportunity to do so.

- 在最後三分之一人生裡，只剩下工作，而單單工作就永遠令人感到刺激、再度年輕、興味昂然與心滿意足。

  For the last third of life there remains only work. It alone is always stimulating, rejuvenating, exciting and satisfying.

- 小說沒有法則，從來就沒有，也永遠不會有。

  There are no laws for the novel. There never have been, nor can there ever be.

# 艾西莫夫 (Isaac Asimov, 1920-1992)

美國20世紀最重要的科幻小說家。19歲正式發表第一篇科幻作品,並開始創作其最著名的《機器人》系列。他的創作力豐沛,產量驚人,一生完成470餘本著作。曾獲5次「雨果獎」與3次「星雲獎」,兩者皆為科幻界的最高榮譽。其科幻小說中最暢銷者還有《銀河帝國》系列、《基地》三部曲以及《機械公敵》等。

● 現今人生最可悲的部分,就是科學累積知識的速度,要快過社會累積智慧。

The saddest aspect of life right now is that science gathers knowledge faster than society gathers wisdom.

● 科幻小說家能預知無可避免之事,雖說問題與災禍恐難避免,解決之道卻不然。

Science fiction writers foresee the inevitable, and although problems and catastrophes may be inevitable, solutions are not.

● 我不相信有所謂的來世,所以我不必花一生來懼怕地獄,或深懼天堂,因為不管地獄的折磨為何,我想天堂的無聊更不堪聞問。

I don't believe in an afterlife, so I don't have to spend my whole life fearing hell, or fearing heaven even more. For whatever the tortures of hell, I think the boredom of heaven would be even worse.

● 活著是樂事,死亡是安息,麻煩的是過度期間。

Life is pleasant. Death is peaceful. It's the transition that's troublesome.

- 為何你們這些物理學家總需要這麼多的昂貴設備？現在數學系除了要錢買紙張、鉛筆、橡皮擦等外，別無所求，而哲學系還更好，連橡皮擦都省了。

  Why is it that you physicists always require so much expensive equipment? Now the Department of Mathematics requires nothing but money for paper, pencils, and erasers...and the Department of Philosophy is better still. It doesn't even ask for erasers.

- 寫作對我而言，只不過是透過手指來思考而已。

  Writing, to me, is simply thinking through my fingers.

- 如果醫師告訴我只能再活六分鐘，我會打字打得快一點。

  If the doctor told me I had six minutes to live, I'd type a little faster.

- 我堅信，自我教育是唯一存在的教育。

  Self-education is, I firmly believe, the only kind of education there is.

- 暴力，是無能之輩最後的避難所。

  Violence is the last refuge of the incompetent.

- 我不怕電腦，就怕沒有電腦。

  I do not fear computers. I fear the lack of them.

# 海勒 (Joseph Heller, 1923-1999)

美國當代重要作家，所寫小說是抗議文學中最具代表性的作品。二次世界大戰期間一度在駐歐空軍服役，執行過60次轟炸任務。戰後曾任《時代》和《展望》等新聞雜誌的文案撰寫員。其成名之作《第22條軍規》（Catch-22），取材於作者自己在戰爭中的親身經歷，該書備獲推崇，1970年被拍成電影。海勒其餘創作尚有《出了毛病》、《像黃金一樣好》等。

- 成功與失敗都有令人難耐的地方，伴隨成功而來的，有嗑藥、離婚、偷情、欺凌、旅遊、冥想、藥物、消沉、神經衰弱以及自殺。伴隨失敗而來的，卻只有失敗。

  Success and failure are both difficult to endure. Along with success come drugs, divorce, fornication, bullying, travel, meditation, medication, depression, neurosis and suicide. With failure comes failure.

- 在走運的時候，命運是可以接受的好事；在走背運的時候，就不必稱它為命運了，應叫它為不公、不義，或就叫它為倒楣好了。

  Destiny is a good thing to accept when it's going your way. When it isn't, don't call it destiny; call it injustice, treachery, or simple bad luck.

- 有些人生來平凡，有些人追求平凡，有些人被強冠以平凡。

  Some men are born mediocre, some men achieve mediocrity, and some men have mediocrity thrust upon them.

- 我不相信奇蹟，因為自有奇蹟以來，已過了好長的時間。

  I don't believe in miracles because it's been a long time since we've had any.

- 何謂國家？一個國家就是四周全以疆界環繞的一片土地，通常並非自然形成。英國人為英國犧牲、美國人為美國犧牲、德國人為德國犧牲、俄國人為俄國犧牲，在這場戰爭（第二次世界大戰）中現有五六十個國家參戰，可想而知，這麼多國家不會全值得為其犧牲。

  What is a country? A country is a piece of land surrounded on all sides by boundaries, usually unnatural. Englishmen are dying for England, Americans are dying for America, Germans are dying for Germany, Russians are dying for Russia. There are now fifty or sixty countries fighting in this war. Surely so many countries can't all be worth dying for.

- 我願保有我的夢，就算是惡夢也好，因為若是無夢可做，漫漫長夜我就無所事事了。

  I want to keep my dreams, even bad ones, because without them, I might have nothing all night long.

- 我所認識的每一個作家，都有寫作上的困擾。

  Every writer I know has trouble writing.

- 當我讀到有人說我一直沒有寫出像《第22條軍規》那樣好的作品時，我很想答說：「又有誰寫出來了？」

  When I read something saying I've not done anything as good as "Catch-22", I'm tempted to reply, "Who has?"

# 安琪洛 ( Maya Angelou, 1928- )

美國著名非洲裔女詩人，應邀於1993年1月20日在克林頓就任總統大典上朗誦就職詩。其詩作以節奏明快、口語化、具吟誦性見稱，成名之作為《只要在我死前給我一口冷水》。1975、1978、1983曾分別出版三本詩集，1986年出版四卷本合集。寫有自傳《我知道籠中之鳥為何會唱歌》。

● 歷史，儘管有其劇痛，卻無法一筆勾消，但若勇敢面對，也就不需要重新來過。

History, despite its wrenching pain, cannot be unlived, but if faced with courage, need not be lived again.

● 我瞭解人們會忘記你說過的話，人們會忘記你做過的事，但是，人們絕不會忘記你給他們的感受。

I've learned that people will forget what you said, people will forget what you did, but people will never forget how you made them feel.

● 做你喜歡的事，才會真正有所成就。不要把金錢當成你的目標，而是去從事你喜歡做的事，好好表現，讓人刮目相看。

You can only become truly accomplished at something you love. Don't make money your goal. Instead, pursue the things you love doing, and then do them so well that people can't take their eyes off you.

● 雖然我知道自己是上帝所造，我也有義務明瞭且銘記其他每個人、每件東西，也都是上帝所創。

While I know myself as a creation of God, I am also obligated to realize and remember that everyone else and everything else are also God's creation.

- 你會遭遇許多挫折，但不可被擊倒。事實上，遭遇挫折或是必需的，如此你才能認識自己，知道你靠什麼翻身，以及如何掙脫挫敗。

  You may encounter many defeats, but you must not be defeated. In fact, it may be necessary to encounter the defeats, so you can know who you are, what you can rise from, how you can still come out of it .

- 愛情，無視於障礙。它跳過柵欄，越過圍籬，穿透高牆，到達充滿希望的終點。

  Love recognizes no barriers. It jumps hurdles, leaps fences, penetrates walls to arrive at it destination full of hope.

- 偏見是一種負荷，困擾著過去，威脅著未來，使現在寸步難行。

  Prejudice is a burden that confuses the past, threatens the future and renders the present inaccessible.

- 勇氣是一切美德中最重要者，因為缺少勇氣，你無法堅守任何其他的美德。

  Courage is the most important of all the virtues, because without courage you can't practice any other virtue consistently.

- 小鳥歡唱不是因為有回應，而是因為心中有歌。

  A bird doesn't sing because it has an answer, it sings because it has a song.

# 維瑟爾 ( Elie Wiesel, 1928- )

當代美國猶太裔作家，1986年諾貝爾和平獎得主。二次大戰期間他被納粹送往集中營，倖免於難。一生藉由創作與演講，關心猶太人與其他同樣遭受迫害族群的處境，於1980-1986年擔任美國大屠殺紀念委員會主席。迄今所完成文學與非文學著作多達40餘本，1985年美國總統雷根頒以國會金質勳章，1992年老布希總統亦授予總統自由勳章。

● 希望，一如和平，不是上帝所賜之禮，而是只能由我們彼此之間互贈的禮物。

Hope is like peace. It is not a gift from God. It is a gift only we can give one another.

● 我覺得書籍就像眾人，各有其命運，有些書引起悲傷，有些書給人喜悅，有些書兼而有之。

I feel that books, just like people, have a destiny. Some invite sorrow, others joy, some both.

● 我還沒有失去對上帝的信心，我雖不免有憤怒與怨懟之時，而也就因如此，有時反而讓我更接近祂。

I have not lost faith in God. I have moments of anger and protest. Sometimes I've been closer to him for that reason.

● 要寫出來，如果不寫你就活不下去的話；要寫出唯獨你能寫出的東西。

Write only if you cannot live without writing. Write only what you alone can write.

● 愛的相反，並不是恨，而是冷漠。

The opposite of love is not hate, it's indifference.

- 由於冷漠，人們在真正死亡之前就已死亡。

  Because of indifference, one dies before one actually dies.

- 我們的義務，就在賦予生命意義，從而征服消極、無謂的人生。

  Our obligation is to give meaning to life and in doing so to overcome the passive, indifferent life.

- 對我而言，冷漠就是邪惡的象徵。

  Indifference, to me, is the epitome of evil.

- 一個正直的人，就能使事情改觀。

  One person of integrity can make a difference.

- 友情給生命所留下的烙痕，甚至更深於愛情；愛情不免陷於糾纏，而友情永遠只在分享。

  Friendship marks a life even more deeply than love. Love risks degenerating into obsession, friendship is never anything but sharing.

# 摩里森 ( Toni Morrison, 1931- )

當代美國最重要的黑人作家。作品曾獲得多項殊榮，包括諾貝爾文學獎、全國書評家協會獎、普立茲文學獎。1970年出版第一部小說《最藍的眼睛》，嶄露頭角，此後陸續推出《蘇拉》、《所羅門之歌》、《黑寶貝》、《寵兒》等四部小說，聲望益隆。1993年榮獲諾貝爾獎，頌辭推崇其作品具有史詩力量，精準呈現美國黑人族裔的生活。

● 所有的水流無不有超好的記憶，永遠都在努力回到其源頭。

All water has a perfect memory and is forever trying to get back to where it was.

● 人生在某一時刻，世間的美已飽和到不需要拍照、繪畫，甚或記憶，就已足夠。

At some point in life the world's beauty becomes enough. You don't need to photograph, paint or even remember it. It is enough.

● 如果有一本書你真想去讀，但卻付之闕如，那麼你就必須把它寫出來。

If there's a book you really want to read, but it hasn't been written yet, then you must write it.

● 我寫出生平第一本小說，因為我想讀它。

I wrote my first novel because I wanted to read it.

● 出生、活著、死亡，都發生在一片樹葉的陰暗面。

Birth, life, and death -- each took place on the hidden side of a leaf.

- 痛苦時，就會拙於言詞，一切痛苦莫不如此。

  When there is pain, there are no words. All pain is the same.


- 世上最孤獨的女人，就是沒有閨中密友的女人。

  The loneliest woman in the world is the woman without a close woman friend.


- 黑人文學被教成社會學、包容之學，而不是嚴肅、精確的藝術形式。

  Black literature is taught as sociology, as tolerance, not as a serious, rigorous art form.


- 解放自己是一回事，主張擁有那個被解放的自己，又當別論。

  Freeing yourself was one thing; claiming ownership of that freed self was another.


- 在這個國家裡，美國人意味著白人，其他每個人都是歸化的美國人。

  In this country American means white. Everybody else has to hyphenate.


- 我不認為一個女人掌家會是問題，會是一個破碎家庭，人們認為它是問題，乃是因為男人為一家之主的觀念作祟。

  I don't think a female running a house is a problem, a broken family. It's perceived as one because of the notion that a head is a man.

# 昆士 (Dean Koontz, 1945- )

美國懸疑小說家。多次榮登《紐約時報》暢銷書排行榜之首，成為榜上之常客，至今已有30餘部作品在全球發行，擁有廣大讀者群。其寫作技巧高超，擅長使書中人物捲入奇特駭人的事件中，故能高潮迭起，引人入勝，《滾石雜誌》譽其為美國最受歡迎的懸疑小說家。作品有《唯一生還者》、《記憶突變》、《地心駭客》等。

- 政客的目標永遠是在操弄公共辯論，我認為雖有一些政客擁有較高的目標，但他們全被權力腐化了。

  A politician's goal is always to manipulate public debate. I think there are some politicians with higher goals. But all of them get corrupted by power.

- 對我而言，書籍是這麼神奇的解脫，因為我可以打開一本書，消失其中，而那是我小時候唯一離家的辦法。

  Books were this wonderful escape for me because I could open a book and disappear into it, and that was the only way out of that house when I was a kid.

- 文明所依賴的，就是事實上多數人在多數時間都會做對的事情。

  Civilization rests on the fact that most people do the right thing most of the time.

- 我不是先寫出草稿，再去修改，而是一頁頁的慢慢幹活，不斷修潤。

  I don't write a quick draft and then revise; instead, I work slowly page by page, revising and polishing.

- 我絕不討論我正在寫的小說，因為害怕一旦談論它，就會削弱我的寫作欲。

  I never discuss a novel while I'm writing it, for fear that talking about it will diminish my desire to write it.

- 我儘量不去花太多時間在政黨政治上，人生太短，無暇顧此。我並不真正相信政治解決過許多人類的問題。

  I try not to spend too much time on partisan politics. Life's too short for that. I don't really believe that there have been many human problems solved by politics.

- 寫小說就像做愛，也像拔牙，苦樂相間，有時它就像拔牙時做愛。

  Writing a novel is like making love, but it's also like having a tooth pulled. Pleasure and pain. Sometimes it's like making love while having a tooth pulled.

- 你的心思總是比一部電影中人們所能顯現的，更要邪門。

  Your mind always does worse things than people can show in a movie.

- 有時世上沒有比我們的心思更為幽暗的地方，那也就是心靈的未央暗夜。

  Sometimes there is no darker place than our thoughts, the moonless midnight of the mind.

# 艾克曼 ( Diane Ackerman, 1948- )

美國著名作家，擅長詩與散文創作，作品多以大自然、心靈探索為主題，獲得世界各地廣大讀者的迴響。曾長期擔任《紐約客》雜誌專欄作家，並在康乃爾、哥倫比亞大學等名校任教。著有《鯨背月色》、《纖細一線間》、《感官之旅》、《愛之旅》、《心靈深戲》、《艾克曼的花園》、《甜笑的美洲虎》及《讚美破壞者》等暢銷之作。

● 我不願意在抵達人生的終點時，才發現我只活過生命的長度，我也要活過生命的廣度才行。

I don't want to get to the end of my life and find that I lived just the length of it. I want to have lived the width of it as well.

● 欠缺了碰觸與被碰觸，所有年齡層的人都會生病，而且變得渴求碰觸。

In the absence of touching and being touched, people of all ages can sicken and grow touch-starved.

● 一首詩紀錄著非一般語言可以形容的情感與情緒，而只能將其連綴在一起，以比喻的方式暗示。

A poem records emotions and moods that lie beyond normal language, that can only be patched together and hinted at metaphorically.

● 人人都承認愛情是美妙與必需的，但愛情究為何物，卻是人言各殊。

Everyone admits that love is wonderful and necessary, yet no one agrees on just what it is.

- 沒有比氣味更令人懷念的，一種氣味可能是無法預期、短暫、飄忽的，卻讓人想起在山中湖畔度過的兒時夏日。

  Nothing is more memorable than a smell. One scent can be unexpected, momentary and fleeting, yet conjure up a childhood summer beside a lake in the mountains.

- 世上有外表體面的笨想法，正如有外表體面的笨蛋一樣。

  There are well-dressed foolish ideas just as there are well-dressed fools.

- 畢竟，咖啡是苦的，它是一種來自禁區與險境的味道。

  After all, coffee is bitter, a flavor from the forbidden and dangerous realm.

- 我不願意在自己的生命裡做一名過客。

  I don't want to be a passenger in my own life.

- 看看你的雙腳，你正站在空中，當我們想到天空時，我們往往會擡頭仰望，然而，天空其實是起始於地面。

  Look at your feet. You are standing in the sky. When we think of the sky, we tend to look up, but the sky actually begins at the earth.

# 村上春樹 (Murakami Haruki, 1949- )

日本小說家、美國文學翻譯家。29歲開始寫作,第一部作品《聽風的歌》獲得日本群像新人賞。1987年長篇小說《挪威的森林》在日本大賣,使其躋身於日本最暢銷的作家之一。2003年《海邊的卡夫卡》英譯本名列紐約時報年度十大好書小說類首位,文壇地位益加穩固。作品尚有《邊境、近境》、《遠方的鼓聲》、《雨天炎天》等。

● 死亡不是生命的相對面,而是生命的一部分。

Death is not the opposite of life, but a part of it.

● 大部分年輕人都往大公司求職,變成公司人,我卻希望做一名個體戶。

Most young people were getting jobs in big companies, becoming company men. I wanted to be individual.

● 沒有所謂「完美的寫作」這回事兒,正如沒有所謂「完美的絕望」一樣。

There's no such thing as perfect writing, just like there's no such thing as perfect despair.

● 正如托爾斯泰所言,快樂是一則諷喻,不快樂是一則故事。

It's like Tolstoy said. Happiness is an allegory, unhappiness a story.

● 回憶溫暖你的內心,但也把你撕裂。

Memories are what warm you up from the inside, but they're also what tear you apart.

- 如果你只讀人人都在讀的書，你也只能思考人人所思考的。

  If you only read the books that everyone else is reading, you can only think what everyone else is thinking.

- 如今我五十五歲了，寫一本書得花三年的時間，我不曉得在我去世前究竟能寫多少本書，這像倒數計時，所以寫每本書時我都祈禱，祈求讓我活著把它完成。

  I am 55 years old now. It takes three years to write one book. I don't know how many books I will be able to write before I die. It is like a countdown. So with each book I am praying - please let me live until I am finished.

- 在日本，人們偏好寫實風格，他們喜歡答案與結論，但我的故事中卻付之闕如，我要讓他們開放於一切可能性，我想我的讀者瞭解那種開放。

  In Japan they prefer the realistic style. They like answers and conclusions, but my stories have none. I want to leave them wide open to every possibility. I think my readers understand that openness.

- 我的爺爺總是說，發問尷尬一時，但不發問卻尷尬一世。

  My grandpa always said that asking questions is embarrassing for a moment, but not asking's embarrassing for a lifetime.

- 打開你的心扉吧，你不是一名囚犯，你是一隻飛翔的鳥，在蒼穹尋夢。

  Unclose your mind. You are not a prisoner. You are a bird in flight, searching the skies for dreams.

# 帕拉尼克 (Chuck Palahniuk, 1961- )

美國小說家和自由撰稿人,以長篇小說處女作《搏擊俱樂部》享譽文壇,作品每每混合了諷刺、喜劇、恐怖以及超現實黑色幽默,風格獨特。多年來,一直是美國《紐約時報》暢銷書排行榜的常客,代表之作如《倖存者》、《看不見的怪獸》、《窒息》、《搖籃曲》、《日記》、《陰魂不散》、《咆哮》等,無不舉世風行。

- 奇怪的是,你怎麼也不會思念你已擁有的女人,你不能忘懷的,永遠是那些離你而去者。

  It's funny how you never think about the women you've had. It's always the ones who get away that you can't forget.

- 人們使用所謂的電話,因為他們討厭膩在一起,卻又害怕孤單。

  People used what they called a telephone because they hated being close together and they were scared of being alone.

- 我們這一代沒遇到大戰爭、大蕭條;我們的戰爭是精神上的,我們的蕭條就是我們的人生。

  Our generation has had no great war, no great depression. Our war is spiritual. Our depression is our lives.

- 上帝所做的一切,就是看守我們,在我們活膩時,取我們的性命,所以我們無論如何都不能活膩。

  All God does is watch us and kill us when we get boring. We must never, ever be boring.

- 一分鐘的完美就值回一切努力，而片刻正是你所能期待於完美的極限。

  A minute of perfection was worth the effort. A moment was the most you could ever expect from perfection.

- 我曾在殯儀館工作，為的是讓自我感覺好一點，也就是認知自己還活著的事實。

  I used to work in a funeral home to feel good about myself, just the fact that I was breathing.

- 我們全都會死，人生的目的不在不朽，而在創造不朽。

  We all die. The goal isn't to live forever, the goal is to create something that will.

- 你有抉擇，生或死，每一呼吸都是一種抉擇，每一分鐘都是一種抉擇，亦即要活下去或不再活。

  You have a choice. Live or die. Every breath is a choice. Every minute is a choice. To be or not to be.

- 如果我能在一個不同的地方、不同的時間睡醒，那麼我能不能以一個不同的人睡醒？

  If I could wake up in a different place, at a different time, could I wake up as a different person?

# 思想界

# 伊比鳩魯 (Epictetus, 55-135)

古羅馬時期斯多噶派的哲學家，曾是奴隸，後恢復自由之身，建立斯多噶派主義學園，以教書終其一生。他接受亞里斯多德學說，倡導心性的實踐，對斯多噶派學說有極其重要的影響，是繼蘇格拉底後西方倫理學說最重要人物之一，對基督教和後來西方哲學的發展亦有深遠影響。

- 要是聽到人家說你的壞話，不必努力辯解，而應說：「他顯然不很瞭解我，因為他可以提到更多其他的缺點。」

  If you hear that someone is speaking ill of you, instead of trying to defend yourself you should say: "He obviously does not know me very well, since there are so many other faults he could have mentioned.

- 大部分時候保持沉默，必要時才發言，而且簡短。

  Keep silence for the most part, and speak only when you must, and then briefly.

- 我們有兩耳一口，所以我們傾聽要比說話多兩倍。

  We have two ears and one mouth so that we can listen twice as much as we speak.

- 一條船不應該仰賴一隻小錨，人生也不應該仰賴單一希望。

  Neither should a ship rely on one small anchor, nor should life rest on a single hope.

- 只有漂亮的身體還不夠，還必須有心靈來搭配。

  It takes more than just a good looking body. You've got to have the heart and soul to go with it.

- 聰明人不會為自己所未擁有的東西苦惱，而是安於自己所擁有的。

  He is a wise man who does not grieve for the things which he has not, but rejoices for those which he has.

- 所謂富有，不在於擁有眾多財產，而是少有需求。

  Wealth consists not in having great possessions, but in having few wants.

- 智者的天性就是抗拒享樂，愚人卻成為享樂的奴隸。

  It is the nature of the wise to resist pleasures, but the foolish to be a slave to them.

- 要想當一名作家，去寫就對了。

  If you wish to be a writer, write.

- 要是你的兄弟對不起你，不要記他的不好，而要銘記他是你的兄弟。

  If thy brother wrongs thee, remember not so much his wrong-doing, but more than ever that he is thy brother.

- 哲學的起源，就是承認意見之間的衝突。

  The beginning of philosophy is the recognition of the conflict between opinions.

# 奧勒利烏斯 (Marcus Aurelius, 121-180)

古羅馬皇帝、哲學家，被視為西羅馬帝國黃金時代的象徵。他在位近二十年，內憂外患不斷，但他仍能以其堅毅的精神勤奮治國，政績斐然。期間頒布眾多法令，使羅馬帝國的法治走上軌道。所著闡釋斯多噶哲學的《沉思錄》，完整記述其宗教觀與道德觀，成為西方世界傳世名著。

- 不要浪費時間去辯論怎樣才算好人，就去做一個好人吧。

  Waste no more time arguing about what a good man should be. Be one.

- 不要活得像有千年可活那樣，而要把每一天都當成生命的末日那樣過。

  Live not one's life as though one had a thousand years, but live each day as the last.

- 你有能力左右你的心，卻無法左右外在的事務，明乎此，你就會找到力量。

  You have power over your mind - not outside events. Realize this, and you will find strength.

- 不要因一件事對你似乎困難，就認定別人也不可能完成。

  Because a thing seems difficult for you, do not think it impossible for anyone to accomplish.

- 一個人所該憂慮的不是死亡，而是他從未開始過活。

  It is not death that a man should fear, but he should fear never beginning to live.

- 早晨起床，想到仍能活著去呼吸、思考、享受、愛，深感何其有幸。

  When you arise in the morning, think of what a precious privilege it is to be alive - to breathe, to think, to enjoy, to love.

- 唯一你能永遠保有的財富，就是你已施捨的財富。

  The only wealth which you will keep forever is the wealth you have given away.

- 一個人的價值，不會超越其抱負。

  A man's worth is no greater than his ambitions.

- 我們的人生，是我們的思想所造成的。

  Our life is what our thoughts make it.

- 生活的藝術，比較像角力，而不像舞蹈。

  The art of living is more like wrestling than dancing.

- 跟自己和諧相處的人，就能跟天地和諧相處。

  He who lives in harmony with himself lives in harmony with the universe.

# 聖耶羅米 ( St. Jerome, 345-420 )

早期西方教會中，學識最淵博的教父，精通古典文學、《聖經》語文和基督教傳統，也是提倡修道院和獨身主義最力之人。他根據希臘《聖經》，把全本聖經譯成拉丁文，此一拉丁版本被定為教會的《聖經》標準本，對中世紀初期學術界影響至巨，而其對《聖經》的註釋和人文主義思想的主張，亦對後世產生深遠影響。

● 務必一直保持忙碌，如此不論什麼時候魔鬼找上門，都會發現你沒空。

Be ever engaged, so that whenever the devil calls he may find you occupied.

● 臉孔是心靈的鏡子，無言的眼睛招認了內心的祕密。

The face is the mirror of the mind, and eyes without speaking confess the secrets of the heart.

● 婚姻對那些害怕夜晚獨眠的人，是有益的。

Marriage is good for those who are afraid to sleep alone at night.

● 會中斷的友情，就絕不是真正的友情。

The friendship that can cease has never been real.

● 朋友要長久尋覓，難以找到，不易保有。

A friend is long sought, hardly found, and with difficulty kept.

- 年過七十，就像參戰。所有的朋友不是風燭殘年，就是已然凋零，我們倖存於陣亡者與彌留者之間，一如身處戰地。

  Being over seventy is like being engaged in a war. All our friends are going or gone and we survive amongst the dead and the dying as on a battlefield.

- 愛情不是用買的，情愛無價。

  Love is not to be purchased, and affection has no price.

- 他們談吐像天使，但生活得像凡人。

  They talk like angels but they live like men.

- 未經裝飾的美，最為奪目。

  Beauty when unadorned is adorned the most.

- 無知於自身的無知，更是可悲。

  It is worse still to be ignorant of your ignorance.

- 別人的疤痕，當讓你提高警覺。

  The scars of others should teach us caution.

# 聖金口若望（Saint John Chrysostom, 347-407）

古代基督教希臘教父、解經家、君士坦丁堡大主教。他是一流的演說家，每次佈道都融入其道德的或社會的教誨，但極少使用諷喻，講經深入淺出，頗具說服力，因此獲得希臘語「金口」(golden-mouthed)的綽號。畢生致力於對貧困受迫者的關懷，備受推崇，著作包括大量的《聖經》講道及其他方面的講道，以及一些論文與書信。

---

● 一位能被瞭解的神，就不是神。

A comprehended god is no god.

---

● 蜜蜂要比其他的動物更受肯定，不是因為她辛勞，而是因為她肯為別人辛勞。

The bee is more honored than other animals, not because she labors, but because she labors for others.

---

● 我知道我自己的靈魂是何等脆弱與渺小，我瞭解這個職務的重要，以及工作的艱鉅；緣以教士的靈魂所遭受驚濤駭浪之侵襲，要多過強風的襲海。

I know my own soul, how feeble and puny it is: I know the magnitude of this ministry, and the great difficulty of the work; for more stormy billows vex the soul of the priest than the gales which disturb the sea.

---

● 財富不受禁止，但對財富的驕傲卻受禁止。

Riches are not forbidden, but the pride of them is.

---

● 真正的豐裕，不是擁有，而是放棄追求財富。

That is true plenty, not to have, but not to want riches.

- 就像蟲蛀衣服一樣，嫉妒會消耗一個人。

  As a moth gnaws a garment, so doth envy consume a man.

- 哲學的最高目標，就是在追求既聰慧又單純，這才是聖潔的人生。

  The highest point of philosophy is to be both wise and simple; this is the angelic life.

- 沒有苦難就不會有安息；沒有冬天就不會有夏天。

  If there were no tribulation, there would be no rest; if there were no winter, there would be no summer.

- 自己不犯錯，別人就奈何不得。

  No one can harm the man who does himself no wrong.

- 地獄是由教士的頭顱所鋪成的。

  Hell is paved with priests' skulls.

# 聖方濟 ( St. Francis of Assisi, 1182-1226 )

義大利傳教士、方濟會和方濟女修會的創始人,因對動物的博愛而被尊為動物和自然生態的守護者,每年訂在10月4日的世界動物日,就是為了紀念此人。他出生富裕之家,成年後為體現基督精神,放棄財產和家庭,堅守清貧。他以身教言教,影響當時日益腐化的教會,幫助人們恢復對教會的信心,故能成為天主教最受愛戴的聖人。

- 在有恨的地方,讓我們播下愛;在有傷害的地方,播下寬恕;在有懷疑的地方,播下信心。

  Where there is hatred, let me sow love. Where there is injury, pardon. Where there is doubt, faith.

- 除非我們能言行一致,否則不管行腳何處去講道,都發揮不了作用。

  It is no use walking anywhere to preach unless our walking is our preaching.

- 在侍奉神時,不宜面露憂傷的面容或冷漠的神色。

  It is not fitting, when one is in God's service, to have a gloomy face or a chilling look.

- 最初要做所必須做的,然後做所可能做的,而突然之間你變成正在做那不可能做的。

  Start by doing what's necessary; then do what's possible; and suddenly you are doing the impossible.

- 唯有寬恕別人,我們才會被人寬恕。

  It is in pardoning that we are pardoned.

- 真正的進步，總是在不知不覺中悄悄挺進。

  True progress quietly and persistently moves along without notice.

- 謀事在人，成事在天。

  Our actions are our own; their consequences belong to Heaven.

- 當我們向上帝祈禱時，我們必須一無所求，一無所求。

  When we pray to God we must be seeking nothing - nothing.

- 我一身汙穢，如果上帝能透過我工作，祂就能透過任何人工作。

  I have been all things unholy. If God can work through me, he can work through anyone.

- 我會做完整理花園的工作。（聖方濟整理花園時，有人問他，如果他突然知道在當天日落前就會死掉，他會做什麼，他這樣回答。）

  I would finish hoeing my garden.

# 聖多瑪斯阿奎那（Saint Thomas Aquinas, 1225-1274）

義大利多米尼克會神學家，是中世紀最重要的經院哲學家，也是天主教正統思想的主要代表，其哲學和神學思想被稱為多瑪斯主義。一生尊崇亞里斯多德，認為亞氏是最偉大的哲學家，所著《神學大全》和《反異教大全》，內容幾乎涵蓋了中世紀神學的所有知識，亦使天主教神學成為經典體系。1323年被追諡為聖徒。

- 對有信仰的人而言，沒有任何解釋是必要的；對沒有信仰的人而言，沒有一種解釋是講得通的。

  To one who has faith, no explanation is necessary. To one without faith, no explanation is possible.

- 信仰，跟看不見的東西有關；希望，跟沒有到手的東西有關。

  Faith has to do with things that are not seen and hope with things that are not at hand.

- 勇氣的首要表現，就在堅定不移地忍受危難，而不是責怪危難。

  The principal act of courage is to endure and withstand dangers doggedly rather than to attack them.

- 追求道德的完美，不是將熱情完全去除，而是加以規範。

  Perfection of moral virtue does not wholly take away the passions, but regulates them.

- 照耀四方，要勝過僅僅發光；散播沉思過的真理，要勝過僅僅沉思。

  Better to illuminate than merely to shine, to deliver to others contemplated truths than merely to contemplate.

- 缺少惡，善可以存在，然而缺少善，惡卻不能存在。

  Good can exist without evil, whereas evil cannot exist without good.

- 假如做一個船長最高的目標就是護船，那麼，他就得把船永遠停靠在港灣裡。

  If the highest aim of a captain were to preserve his ship, he would keep it in port forever.

- 人的救贖要靠三件事：知道他所應相信的、知道他所應渴望的、知道他所應去做的。

  Three things are necessary for the salvation of man: to know what he ought to believe; to know what he ought to desire; and to know what he ought to do.

- 如果你在尋找你應走之路，就選基督吧，因為基督本身就是道路。

  If, then, you are looking for the way by which you should go, take Christ, because He Himself is the way.

- 睡個好覺、洗個澡、喝杯葡萄酒，可使悲傷減輕。

  Sorrow can be alleviated by good sleep, a bath and a glass of wine.

# 馬丁路德 (Martin Luther, 1483-1546)

德國傳教士、宗教學者和語言學家，亦是基督新教在信仰和制度等方面的主要奠基人。他花了十二年時間將聖經譯為德文，使聖經在西歐普及化，對西歐的文化發展影響深遠。所領導的宗教改革運動，不僅促使各種不同新興教派陸續誕生，也引發歐洲後來的宗教戰爭。一生著作等身，內容多與宗教活動有關，也充分反映其哲學思想和宗教理論。

● 神不只是把福音寫在聖經裡，也把它寫在樹木、花朵、雲彩與星辰之上。

God writes the gospel not in the Bible alone, but on trees, and flowers, and clouds, and stars.

● 信仰是對神的恩典具有一種真正、無畏的信心，是如此的確信與確定，可以用自己的生命押注千百回。

Faith is a living, daring confidence in God's grace, so sure and certain that a man could stake his life on it a thousand times.

● 一個傳道人，必須既是軍人，也是牧羊人。他必須助長、保衛與教導；他必須口中有牙，能咬能打。

A preacher must be both soldier and shepherd. He must nourish, defend, and teach; he must have teeth in his mouth, and be able to bite and fight.

● 人心就像是怒海中的一隻船，受四面襲來的天風驅策。

The human heart is like a ship on a stormy sea driven about by winds blowing from all four corners of heaven.

- 你不僅要對你所說的負責，也應該為你所沒說的負責。

  You are not only responsible for what you say, but also for what you do not say.

- 末了，我們不會記得敵人講的話，只會記得朋友的沉默。

  In the End, we will remember not the words of our enemies, but the silence of our friends.

- 要祈禱，讓上帝去煩惱。

  Pray, and let God worry.

- 如果天堂裡不准笑，我不想去那兒。

  If you're not allowed to laugh in heaven, I don't want to go there.

- 主常常把財富賜給笨蛋，不給他們其他任何東西。

  The Lord commonly gives riches to foolish people, to whom he gives nothing else.

- 理性是信仰的敵人。

  Reason is the enemy of faith.

# 葛拉西安 (Baltasar Gracian, 1601-1658)

17世紀西班牙哲學家、思想家、宗教家，有人文主義大師之稱。18歲時進入耶穌會見習修行，歷任軍中神父、告解神父、教授等職。《英雄寶鏡》與《智慧書》是其傳世之作，德國哲學家叔本華對後者尤為推崇，將其譯成德文，而尼采也盛讚此書論述精闢。葛氏的預言小說《批評大師》，則是西班牙最著名的諷刺文學。

- 男人在二十歲是孔雀，三十是獅子，四十是駱駝，五十是蛇，六十是狗，七十是猴，八十什麼也不是。

  At 20 a man is a peacock, at 30 a lion, at 40 a camel, at 50 a serpent, at 60 a dog, at 70 an ape, and at 80 nothing.

- 聰明人從敵人身上所獲得的益處，多過笨蛋從朋友身上所獲得的。

  A wise man gets more use from his enemies than a fool from his friends.

- 不少人的偉大，是由其敵人所造就。

  Many have had their greatness made for them by their enemies.

- 把祕密透露給別人，就會使自己淪為對方的奴隸。

  He that communicates his secret to another makes himself that other's slave.

- 怒氣沖沖時絕不要輕舉妄動，因為你將動輒出錯。

  Never do anything when you are in a temper, for you will do everything wrong.

- 我們記得最清楚的事，是那些最該忘記的。

  The things we remember best are those better forgotten.

- 美人應儘早打破她的鏡子。

  A beautiful woman should break her mirror early.

- 與其獨自清醒，不如與世人一起瘋狂。

  Better mad with the rest of the world than wise alone.

- 絕不要跟一個一無可失的人爭辯。

  Never contend with a man who has nothing to lose.

- 真正的知識，就在於通達生活之道。

  True knowledge lies in knowing how to live.

- 缺少了勇氣，智慧無從結出果實。

  Without courage, wisdom bears no fruit.

## 畢奇爾 ( Henry Ward Beecher, 1813-1887 )

美國著名佈道家、演說家、19世紀支援廢奴主義的代表性
人物。一生以傳道為職志，極喜接觸會眾，週日之佈道，
動輒吸引數千人與會，其盛況可見一斑，林肯總統稱他為
「自古以來最多產的心靈。」畢氏述而不作，所出版之講
道集，大部分是由別人記錄下來而由其修訂而成。

● 基督徒不過是一名罪人，他真心向善，自願接受基督的洗禮。

A Christian is nothing but a sinful man who has put himself
to school for Christ for the honest purpose of becoming
better.

● 如果一個人不能在自己所在的地方做基督徒，那麼他在哪裡都
不能成為基督徒。

If a man cannot be a Christian in the place where he is, he
cannot be a Christian anywhere.

● 每一項善行都是邁向天堂的踏腳石。

Every charitable act is a stepping stone toward heaven.

● 每個明天都有二個柄，我們要握住它，可以用「焦慮之柄」，
或用「信心之柄」。

Every tomorrow has two handles. We can take hold of it
with the handle of anxiety or the handle of faith.

● 驕傲的人很少會是感恩的人，因為他永不會滿足於自己所應得
的。

A proud man is seldom a grateful man, for he never thinks
he gets as much as he deserves.

- 我可以原諒，但我不能忘記，只是我不原諒的另一種說法。原諒應像是一張註銷的票據，一撕兩半，付之一炬，如此再也不能做不利對方的提示。

  I can forgive, but I cannot forget, is only another way of saying, I will not forgive. Forgiveness ought to be like a cancelled note - torn in two, and burned up, so that it never can be shown against one.

- 眼淚常是望遠鏡，人們用它眺望天堂。

  Tears are often the telescope by which men see far into heaven.

- 要是一個國家的年輕人都是保守派，這個國家的喪鐘已響。

  When a nation's young men are conservative, its funeral bell is already rung.

- 年輕之愛是火燄，非常美，往往非常熱與猛，但仍只不過是光芒閃爍而已。年長及有所節制的愛，就像煤炭，深深燃燒，不可扼抑。

  Young love is a flame; very pretty, often very hot and fierce, but still only light and flickering. The love of the older and disciplined heart is as coals, deep-burning, unquenchable.

- 真正的順服，才是真正的自由。

  True obedience is true freedom.

# 司布真 (Charles Haddon Spurgeon, 1834-1892)

19世紀英國著名牧師，有講道王子之稱，其佈道集及著作至今仍廣泛流傳。司氏一生出版有宣道文章達三千餘篇，計75冊。另出版書籍135部，其中最著名者，係詩篇的注釋《大衛三寶藏》以及《早晚靈修》兩部書。司氏講道之特點，即是精選合乎神旨的題材，用「以經解經」的方法加以宣揚，極具說服力與感染力。

- 在天堂中沒有一個頭戴冠冕的人，在世時不是背負十字架者。

  There are no crown-wearers in heaven that were not cross-bearers here below.

- 好的品格是至上的墓碑。那些愛你的人以及你幫過的人，即使在「勿忘我之花」枯萎後，仍會記得你。要把你的名字刻在別人心中，而不是刻在大理石上。

  A good character is the best tombstone. Those who loved you, and were helped by you, will remember you when forget-me-nots are withered. Carve your name on hearts, and not on marble.

- 造就快樂的，不是我們擁有多少，而是我們享受多少。

  It is not how much we have, but how much we enjoy, that makes happiness.

- 有人說，諾亞方舟若是由一票人建造，可能迄未裝上龍骨。有可能如此，凡事若是眾人之事，就不是任何人之事。世間最偉大的事物，無不是由個人所獨力完成。

  It is said that if Noah's ark had to be built by a company, they would not have laid the keel yet; and it may be so. What is many men's business is nobody's business. The greatest things are accomplished by individual men.

- 智慧乃是知識的正確使用，有知識並不等於有智慧，不少人知道的很多，卻因而冥頑不靈，世上最愚不可及的，就是有知識的笨蛋。瞭解如何使用知識，才算擁有了智慧。

  Wisdom is the right use of knowledge. To know is not to be wise. Many men know a great deal, and are all the greater fools for it. There is no fool so great a fool as a knowing fool. But to know how to use knowledge is to have wisdom.

- 通往智慧殿堂的門階，就是認知我們自己的無知。

  The doorstep to the temple of wisdom is the knowledge of our own ignorance.

- 隔牆有耳，你不想上報的東西，就須三緘其口。

  No one knows who is listening, say nothing you would not wish put in the newspapers.

- 真誠，使凡夫俗子變得比有才華的偽君子更有價值。

  Sincerity makes the very least person to be of more value than the most talented hypocrite.

- 窮人裝闊，最是可悲。

  No one is so miserable as the poor person who maintains the appearance of wealth.

# 慕迪 (Dwight L. Moody, 1837-1899)

美國十九世紀著名佈道家，其講道以單純有力、直指人心
著稱，每每振臂呼籲信眾悔改，極具感染力。一生奔波各
地宣道，深獲教友愛戴，創立有「慕迪聖經學院」，培育
無數宣教人才。在其離世前留有遺言：「當諸位在報紙上
看到我的死訊，千萬不要相信，因為那時我已跨進永生不
死之所」，由此可見其信仰之堅定不移。

● 最能為《聖經》辯護的書，莫過於《聖經》本身。

There's no better book with which to defend the Bible than
the Bible itself.

● 我們之中有許多人都願意為主去做大事，但我們之中卻少有人
願意去做小事。

There are many of us that are willing to do great things for
the Lord, but few of us are willing to do little things.

● 多年來我一直奉為圭臬的是：把主耶穌基督視為個人的朋友。
祂的存在不是一種信念，一種教條而已，我們所擁有的，其實
就是基督本身。

A rule I have had for years is: to treat the Lord Jesus Christ
as a personal friend. His is not a creed, a mere doctrine,
but it is He Himself we have.

● 我們談論天堂的遙遠，但對屬於那兒的人來說，天堂近在咫
尺。天堂是給已預備好的人所預備的地方。

We talk about heaven being so far away. It is within
speaking distance to those who belong there. Heaven is a
prepared place for a prepared people.

- 有人叫我們要讓燈火通明，其實它若是亮著，也就不需告訴任何人它的存在。燈塔不會開砲去引人注意其發光，它們只是默默照射著。

  We are told to let our light shine, and if it does, we won't need to tell anybody it does. Lighthouses don't fire cannons to call attention to their shining- they just shine.

- 《聖經》使你遠離罪惡，或說罪惡使你遠離《聖經》。

  The Bible will keep you from sin, or sin will keep you from the Bible.

- 神絕不會做一種美好到不會實現的承諾。

  God never made a promise that was too good to be true.

- 所謂品德，就是在黑暗中你的所做所為。

  Character is what you are in the dark.

- 好的榜樣，要遠勝過好的訓誨。

  A good example is far better than a good precept.

# 依禮士 ( Henry Ellis, 1859-1939 )

英國性心理學泰斗，與性學大師佛洛依德齊名。他的煌煌巨著《性心理學研究》，是心理醫師與心理學者必讀的經典。1894年，其首部探討兩性問題的著作《男與女》問世，奠定了他的學術地位，內中對性心理取向對性生活品質的影響，頗多闡釋。主要著作尚有《性的道德》、《性的教育》、《性心理學》等。

● 唯獨偉人最是好色，他們要是不敢好色，也就絕不敢變得偉大了。

It is only the great men who are truly obscene. If they had not dared to be obscene, they could never have dared to be great.

● 痛苦與死亡都是人生一部分，排斥它們，就等於排斥人生本身。

Pain and death are part of life. To reject them is to reject life itself.

● 夢只要存續著，就是真實的，我們對生命還能再說些什麼？

Dreams are real as long as they last. Can we say more of life?

● 上帝所應許之地，永遠是存在於荒野的另一邊。

The Promised Land always lies on the other side of a Wilderness.

● 要做眾人的領袖，就必須背向眾人。

To be a leader of men one must turn one's back on men.

- 我們所謂的「道德」，只是對戒律的盲從而已。

  What we call "morals" is simply blind obedience to words of command.


- 一切生活藝術，就在於「放手」與「保留」的妥善混合。

  All the art of living lies in a fine mingling of letting go and holding on.


- 每一位藝術家都在寫他個人的自傳。

  Every artist writes his own autobiography.


- 瞭解自己的人，不再是笨蛋，他們站在智慧之門的門檻。

  Men who know themselves are no longer fools. They stand on the threshold of the door of Wisdom.


- 人靠想像而活。

  Man lives by imagination.


- 副產品有時比產品更有價值。

  The byproduct is sometimes more valuable than the product.


- 毫無瑕疵的美，本身就是一種瑕疵。

  The absence of flaw in beauty is itself a flaw.

# 福斯迪克 （Harry Emerson Fosdick, 1878-1969）

美國著名傳道人、教師、作家。講道時，喜採用大量人生經驗作為材料，使他成為當代最受歡迎的宗教發言人之一。1919年擔任紐約第一長老會牧師，每逢講道，聽眾滿堂，但為保守派所斥責。後擔任派克大道教會牧師，建議在哥倫比亞大學附近建立各派聯合教堂，獲得小洛克斐勒的資助，此一樓高22層的教堂，落成於1926年。

- 宗教不是負荷，不是重擔，而是翅膀。

  Religion is not a burden, not a weight, it is wings.

- 馬不加韁，無處可去；水流或氣體不受限，無法推進物體；尼加拉河不引流，不能轉化成燈光及動能；人生若不聚焦、專注、受到制約，無法成就偉大。

  No horse gets anywhere until he is harnessed. No stream or gas drives anything until it is confined. No Niagara is ever turned into light and power until it is tunneled. No life ever grows great until it is focused, dedicated, disciplined.

- 選擇道路起點的人，就等於選擇了道路通往之地。這就是說，方法決定了結果。

  He who chooses the beginning of the road chooses the place it leads to. It is the means that determines the end.

- 講道，是以團體為基礎的個人諮商。

  Preaching is personal counseling on a group basis.

- 不管你嘲笑別人甚麼，嘲笑自己再說。

  Whatever you laugh at in others, laughs at yourself.

- 我寧願活在一個神祕環繞於人生的世界，也不願活在一個小到我內心可以理解的世界。

  I would rather live in a world where my life is surrounded by mystery than live in a world so small that my mind could comprehend it.

- 我們無法全都變得偉大，但是我們總可以依附某些偉大的事物。

  We cannot all be great, but we can always attach ourselves to something that it great.

- 憎恨他人，就像是為了滅鼠而去燒掉自己的房子一樣。

  Hating people is like burning down your own house to get rid of a rat.

- 民主，是植基於堅信普通人身上也有不凡的可能性。

  Democracy is based upon the conviction that there are extraordinary possibilities in ordinary people.

- 自由總是危險的，但那卻是我們所擁有最安全的東西了。

  Liberty is always dangerous, but it is the safest thing we have.

# 賀佛爾 （Eric Hoffer, 1902-1983）

美國哲學家，以撰寫有關人生、權力和社會秩序的著作而聞名。生平第一部作品《真正的信仰者》（The True Believer），闡釋他對群眾運動的見解，析論深刻精闢，一舉成名。其他著作如《心靈的情感狀態》、《變化的考驗》、《在江畔的工作與思考》、《安息日前》等，皆獲好評。曾長期為《舊金山檢查人報》撰寫專欄，備受推崇。1982年，榮獲象徵美國公民最高榮譽的總統自由勳章。

- 做領袖的必須務實，做個現實主義者，但也必須高談願景，做個理想主義者。

  The leader has to be practical and a realist, yet must talk the language of the visionary and the idealist.

- 擁有絕對權力的人，不僅會預言，使預言成真，而且也會說謊，使謊言成真。

  Those in possession of absolute power can not only prophesy and make their prophecies come true, but they can also lie and make their lies come true.

- 在急遽變動的時代，承繼未來的會是初學者，有學問的人往往發現自己只配活在一個已不存在的世界。

  In a time of drastic change it is the learners who inherit the future. The learned usually find themselves equipped to live in a world that no longer exists.

- 從觀察敵人用來威脅你的手段，你可以發現什麼是敵人最懼怕的東西。

  You can discover what your enemy fears most by observing the means he uses to frighten you.

- 我們所做的最大掩飾，不是遮掩內心的邪惡與醜陋，而是自己的空虛，世上最難遮掩的，就是不存在的東西。

  Our greatest pretenses are built up not to hide the evil and the ugly in us, but our emptiness. The hardest thing to hide is something that is not there.

- 愛整個人類，要比愛鄰居來得容易。

  It is easier to love humanity as a whole than to love one's neighbor.

- 宣傳不會欺騙人們，它只是幫人們欺騙自己而已。

  Propaganda does not deceive people; it merely helps them to deceive themselves.

- 世上沒有比失敗者的孤獨更為孤獨的東西，失敗者連在自己的家裡都成了陌生人。

  There is no loneliness greater than the loneliness of a failure. The failure is a stranger in his own house.

- 只有對我們不瞭解的事物，我們才會有絕對的把握。

  We can be absolutely certain only about things we do not understand.

- 青春本身就是一種才情，一種易逝的才情。

  Youth itself is a talent, a perishable talent.

# 葛拉瑟 (William Glasser, 1925- )

美國心理治療學家。認為傳統的精神分析治療有極大侷限性，而首創現實治療法（Reality Therapy），主張人們不是受外在世界的存在方式影響，而是受自身知覺方式的左右，因此，心理治療應以當事人的主觀世界為核心。著作有《現實治療法》、《認同的社會》、《心理的運作》等。

● 我們所做的每一件事，不管是好是壞，在那當下都是最好的選擇。

Good or bad, everything we do is our best choice at that moment.

● 大多數人心頭都縈繞著「性」，特別是那些不應擁有性愛的人。

Sex is on the minds of most people, especially those who shouldn't be having it.

● 如果你想改變態度，就應從改變行為開始。

If you want to change attitudes, start with a change in behavior.

● 我們被五種基因上的需求所驅使：生存、愛與歸屬感、權力、自由，以及玩樂。

We are driven by five genetic needs: survival, love and belonging, power, freedom, and fun.

● 在乎對方，但卻絕不企圖擁有，可說是去界定友情的深層方式。

Caring for but never trying to own may be a further way to define friendship.

- 我們學得10%所讀到的、20%所聽到的、30%所看到的、50%所看到及聽到的、70%所討論到的；80%所經歷到的；95%所教別人的。

  We learn 10% of what we read; 20% of what we hear; 30% of what we see; 50% of what we see and hear; 70% of what we discuss; 80% of what we experience; 95% of what we teach others.


- 不能為友的人不可結為連理，如果你們之間還無性關係的話。

  Don't marry someone you would not be friends with if there was no sex between you.


- 你走得愈快，拋在你後面的學生就愈多，所以你教多少或多快倒沒啥關係，真正的評量是，學生究竟學得了多少。

  The faster you go, the more students you leave behind. It doesn't matter how much or how fast you teach. The true measure is how much students have learned.


- 痛苦的過去發生了何事，跟今日的我們固然息息相關，但重返此一痛苦的過去，對現在我們所需做的，卻無多大助益。

  What happened in the past that was painful has a great deal to do with what we are today, but revisiting this painful past can contribute little or nothing to what we need to do now.


- 每個人都需要一名不可或缺的朋友。

  Everybody needs one essential friend.

# 舒勒（Robert H. Schuller, 1926- ）

美國基督新教牧師、電視福音主義者。創辦由教堂主持的24小時預防自殺熱線，數百萬人通過熱線獲得牧師諮詢。另開辦有電視廣播節目《力量時刻》，每週約3,000萬人收看此一節目。他積極籌建玻璃式建築，此即為著名的水晶宮大教堂。迄今已完成30多本勵志書，其中6本名列《紐約時報》和《出版人週刊》暢銷書排行榜。

● 正如我們變成獨特的個體一樣，我們也要學著尊重別人的獨特處。

As we grow as unique persons, we learn to respect the uniqueness of others.

● 你往往可以用夢想的大小，來衡量一個人。

You can often measure a person by the size of his dream.

● 很難說什麼是不可能的，因為昨日的夢想就是今日的希望，以及明日的現實。

It is difficult to say what is impossible, for the dream of yesterday is the hope of today and the reality of tomorrow.

● 從事任何事業最缺乏的，不是金錢，而是想法。如果想法不錯，現金總會流到所需之處。

Our greatest lack is not money for any undertaking, but rather ideas, If the ideas are good, cash will somehow flow to where it is needed.

● 上帝的延遲，不等於上帝的否決。

God's delays are not God's denials.

- 失敗並不意謂你是失敗的人，只意謂你尚未成功。

  Failure doesn't mean you are a failure it just means you haven't succeeded yet.

- 如果不存在著失敗的可能，勝利也就毫無意義了。

  If there exists no possibility of failure, then victory is meaningless.

- 讓你的希望，而非你的傷痛，來塑造你的未來。

  Let your hopes, not your hurts, shape your future.

- 永遠要珍視你還擁有的，絕不要注意你所失去的。

  Always look at what you have left. Never look at what you have lost.

- 今日的成就，是昨日的不可能。

  Today's accomplishments were yesterday's impossibilities.

- 人生只是片刻，死亡也不過是另一個片刻。

  Life is but a moment, death also is but another.

# 羅恩 ( Jim Rohn, 1930- )

美國著名商業哲學家、研究成功學的先驅，被譽為最能鼓舞人心的人生導航師。經常為頂級的銷售組織和管理團體開辦培訓課程，三、四十年間舉辦過6,000場次的演講，學員遍及全球，總數超過四百萬人次。著作有《向成功挑戰》、《生命拼圖的五大塊》、《致富與快樂的七大策略》、《邁向偉大的三把鑰匙》等十七本暢銷書。

- 讓別人過渺小的一生，但不是你；讓別人為小事爭執，但不是你；讓別人為小傷痛哭號，但不是你；讓別人把未來交在他人手上，但不是你。

  Let others lead small lives, but not you. Let others argue over small things, but not you. Let others cry over small hurts, but not you. Let others leave their future in someone else's hands, but not you.

- 要解決任何麻煩，不妨問自己三個問題：第一，我可以做什麼事？第二，我可以讀什麼書？第三，我可以向誰請教？

  To solve any problem, here are three questions to ask yourself: First, what could I do? Second, what could I read? And third, who could I ask?

- 領導統禦的正確目標，就是幫那些不會做事的人把事情做好，而也要幫那些會做事的人把事情做得甚至更好。

  A good objective of leadership is to help those who are doing poorly to do well and to help those who are doing well to do even better.

- 正規的教育，使你得以謀生；自我的教育，使你發財。

  Formal education will make you a living; self-education will make you a fortune.

- 個性，並非和指紋一樣的與生俱來，無法改變。個性不是天生的，你必須為它的養成負起責任。

  Character isn't something you were born with and can't change, like your fingerprints. It's something you weren't born with and must take responsibility for forming.

- 失敗不是單一的災變，你並非失敗於一夕之間，而是日復一日的做出一些錯誤的判斷。

  Failure is not a single, cataclysmic event. You don't fail overnight. Instead, failure is a few errors in judgment, repeated every day.

- 所謂成功，就是把平常的事做得有聲有色。

  Success is doing ordinary things extraordinarily well.

- 善用每一個機會去練習你的溝通技巧，如此一旦遇上重要場合，你就會有感動他人的才能、格調、敏銳、清晰以及情感。

  Take advantage of every opportunity to practice your communication skills so that when important occasions arise, you will have the gift, the style, the sharpness, the clarity, and the emotions to affect other people.

- 必要時，可以錯過一餐，但不可錯過一本書。

  Miss a meal if you have to, but don't miss a book.

# 社會賢達

# 赫胥黎 ( Thomas Huxley, 1825-1925 )

英國著名博物學家，因捍衛進化論而有「達爾文的堅定追隨者」之稱。一生發表過150多篇科學論文，內容包括動物學、植物學、生物學、地質學以及人類學等領域。中國近代翻譯家嚴復在清末首先譯述了赫氏部分著作，取名為《天演論》，以「物競天擇，適者生存」的觀點倡導國人救亡圖存，對當時中國思想界產生極大影響。

● 歷史警告我們，對於新出爐的真理，其宿命是起初被當成異端，末了被當成迷信。

History warns us that it is the customary fate of new truths to begin as heresies and to end as superstitions.

● 對人體貼、慷慨、謙和、自重，是造就真正紳士或淑女的特質。

Thoughtfulness for others, generosity, modesty, and self-respect are the qualities which make a real gentleman or lady.

● 人生最可悲的事之一就是，若要設法讓人快樂，很難成竹在胸，但要讓人不快樂，幾乎總可十拿九穩。

It is one of the most saddening things in life that, try as we may, we can never be certain of making people happy, whereas we can almost always be certain of making them unhappy.

● 科學與文學不是兩碼子事，而是一事的兩面。

Science and literature are not two things, but two sides of one thing.

- 對一切事物多少都要去瞭解一點，而對某一事物卻要能瞭解其一切。

  Try to learn something about everything and everything about something.

- 苦難，是一根永不熄滅的火柴。

  Misery is a match that never goes out.

- 世上最堅強的人，就是那種孑然屹立者。

  The strongest man in the world is the man who stands alone.

- 無知的熱心，等於是無光的火燄。

  Zeal without knowledge is fire without light.

- 時間，對真理無能為力，卻將其餘一切啃蝕殆盡。

  Time, whose tooth gnaws away at everything else, is powerless against truth.

- 要緊的不是誰對，而是什麼是對的。

  It is not who is right, but what is right, that is of importance.

- 所謂科學，只不過是有訓練、有組織的常識而已。

  Science is nothing but trained and organized common sense.

# 丹諾（Clarence Darrow, 1857-1938）

美國當代最偉大的律師之一，曾在許多重大刑事審判案件中擔任被告辯護人。一生矢志為無助的弱勢團體與窮人辯護，其庭辯演說往往能撼動人心，使公理正義獲得伸張，亦使其個人得以在美國法律史上佔有一席之地。著作除自傳外，尚有《波斯珍珠》、《抗拒並非罪惡》、《以牙還牙》、《無神論與異教徒》等。

● 歷史會重演，而那也就是歷史的毛病之一。

History repeats itself, and that's one of the things that's wrong with history.

● 正義跟法庭中所進行的事無關，正義是法庭所出來的東西。

Justice has nothing to do with what goes on in a courtroom; justice is what comes out of a courtroom.

● 世上沒有正義這種東西，不管是在法庭內或法庭外。

There is no such thing as justice - in or out of court.

● 法律該像衣服，應為其服務的人群量身制定。

Laws should be like clothes. They should be made to fit the people they serve.

● 一個人在二十歲時滿懷鬥志與希望，想要改造世界；到了七十歲，他仍想改造世界，但他知道自己無能為力。

At twenty a man is full of fight and hope. He wants to reform the world. When he is seventy he still wants to reform the world, but he knows he can't.

- 對真理的追求，讓你活得海闊天空，縱使你永難與真理並駕齊驅。

  The pursuit of truth will set you free; even if you never catch up with it.

- 經由保護他人的自由，你才能在這世上保護自己的自由。

  You can only protect your liberties in this world by protecting the other man's freedom.

- 我因被人誤解而受苦，但我若被人瞭解，恐怕已受更多的苦。

  I have suffered from being misunderstood, but I would have suffered a hell of a lot more if I had been understood.

- 假如你失去笑的力量，你就失去思考的力量。

  If you lose the power to laugh, you lose the power to think.

- 不景氣讓人接近教堂，但葬禮亦能如此。

  Depressions may bring people closer to the church but so do funerals.

- 我從未殺過人，但不少訃告讀來讓我極感快慰。

  I have never killed a man, but I have read many obituaries with great pleasure.

# 凱特寧 (Charles Kettering, 1876-1958)

美國20世紀初期著名的發明家，不少人將凱氏與發明家愛迪生相提並論。他所發明的電子啟動器，使汽車駕駛變得輕鬆方便。此一發明在凱迪拉克1912車型上首次使用，至今仍被公認為二十世紀最重要的汽車創新。去世時，已擁有140餘項發明專利，30多間大學授予榮譽博士學位。

● 發明家，只不過是不把自身的教育看得太重的人。

An inventor is simply a fellow who doesn't take his education too seriously.

● 失敗並不丟臉，失敗是世上最偉大的藝術之一。

It is not a disgrace to fail. Failing is one of the greatest arts in the world.

● 知道並不等於瞭解，知道與瞭解之間有重大差異，對某一事物，你可以知道得很多，卻不是真正對它有所瞭解。

Knowing is not understanding. There is a great difference between knowing and understanding: you can know a lot about something and not really understand it.

● 人們把發明家當成怪人，但沒人問過發明家是怎麼想其他人的。

People think of the inventor as a screwball, but no one ever asks the inventor what he thinks of other people.

● 只要有開放的心與積極的手，就永遠有可開拓的新境界。

There will always be a frontier where there is an open mind and a willing hand.

- 如果你一直想著昨天的事，就不可能擁有一個較好的明天。

  You can't have a better tomorrow if you are thinking about yesterday all the time.

- 抱持著信念去行動吧，就好像它不可能失敗一樣。

  Believe and act as if it were impossible to fail.

- 我關心未來，因為我將在那兒度過餘生。

  My interest is in the future because I am going to spend the rest of my life there.

- 問題敘述清楚，就等於把問題解決了一半。

  A problem well stated is a problem half solved.

- 重要的是，不是我們知道什麼，而是什麼是我們所不知道的。

  It is not what we know that is important, it is what we do not know.

- 所謂研究，意味著你有所不知，卻願意尋求解答。

  Research means that you don't know, but are willing to find out.

# 菲爾普斯 ( Michael Phelps, 1985- )

美國當今最出色的全能型游泳選手。15歲時崛起於泳壇，成為美國奧運泳隊中最年輕的選手。他是多項游泳世界紀錄保持者，也是奧運會奪金紀錄保持者。在2008年北京奧運會上，一舉打破7項世界紀錄，奪得8面金牌，締造了世界泳壇和奧運史上的奇蹟。2003年榮獲有「美國體育界奧斯卡」之稱的沙利文獎。

● 有機會在游泳史上佔一席之地，並把此項運動帶至一個新的境界，將是我的榮幸。努力一拚，此其時也。

I have the opportunity to be part of swimming history. To take the sport to a new level would be an honor for me. There's no better time to try this than now.

● 我認為天下沒有不可能的事，只要你專心一意，付出心血與時間；我認為你的心靈真能控制一切。

I think that everything is possible as long as you put your mind to it and you put the work and time into it. I think your mind really controls everything.

● 我要在回顧時能說：「我已盡全力，而且成功了。」我可不要在回顧時說，我應該如何如何，我要為未來年輕一代的泳手有所變革。

I want to be able to look back and say, "I've done everything I can, and I was successful." I don't want to look back and say I should have done this or that. I'd like to change things for the younger generation of swimmers coming along.

● 我不願預測歷史，但世上沒有什麼不可能的事。

I won't predict anything historic. But nothing is impossible.

- 我要測試我的極限，看看能做到多少，我想改變游泳的世界。

  I want to test my maximum and see how much I can do. And I want to change the world of swimming.

- 我若沒有游出我的最佳成績，我在上課時、在吃晚飯時，以及跟朋友在一起時，都會想著這檔事，那簡直要把我逼瘋。

  If I didn't swim my best, I'd think about it at school, at dinner, with my friends. It would drive me crazy.

- 我的目標就是奧林匹克金牌，世上沒有多少人能說：「我是奧林匹克金牌得主。」

  My goal is one Olympic gold medal. Not many people in this world can say, "I'm an Olympic gold medalist."

- 游泳是我日常必做之事，我感到放鬆、自在，我熟知環境，它就是我的家。

  Swimming is normal for me. I'm relaxed. I'm comfortable, and I know my surroundings. It's my home.

- 你不能為任何事設限，你夢想得愈多，就走得愈遠。

  You can't put a limit on anything. The more you dream, the farther you get.

- 我要改變游泳這項運動，要人們談論它、想到它、期盼看它。

  I want to change the sport of swimming. I want people to talk about it, think about it, and look forward to seeing it.

# 九歌最新叢書

◎定價如有調整，請以各該書新版版權頁定價為準。
◎購書方法：
　・單冊郵購八五折，大量訂購，另有優待辦法。
　・如以信用卡購書，請電（或傳真 02-25789205）索信用卡
　　購書單。
　・網路訂購：九歌文學網：www.chiuko.com.tw
　・郵政劃撥：0112295-1　九歌出版社有限公司
　・電洽客服部：02-25776564 分機 9

九歌文庫 940

# 世界名人智慧菁華・中英對照

輯譯　　　　王壽來

責任編輯　　陳逸華

發行人　　　蔡文甫

出版發行　　九歌出版社有限公司

　　　　　　臺北市105八德路3段12巷57弄40號

　　　　　　電話／02-25776564・傳真／02-25789205

　　　　　　郵政劃撥／0112295-1

九歌文學網　www.chiuko.com.tw

印刷　　　　晨捷印製股份有限公司

法律顧問　　龍躍天律師・蕭雄淋律師・董安丹律師

初版　　　　2010（民國99）年11月

定價　　　　**240元**

書號　　　　F0940

ISBN　　　　978-957-444-735-0

（缺頁、破損或裝訂錯誤，請寄回本公司更換）

國家圖書館出版品預行編目資料

世界名人智慧菁華‧中英對照／王壽來輯譯.
－ 初版. -- 臺北市：九歌, 民99.11

面；　公分. -- (九歌文庫 ; 940)

ISBN 978-957-444-735-0(平裝)

192.8　　　　　　　　　　　　99020073

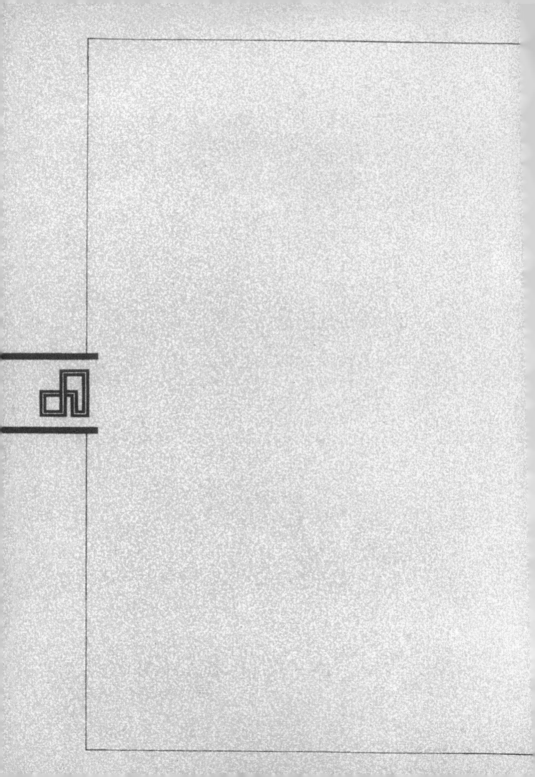